Doo
Entryways

WILLIAM P. SPENCE

Sterling Publishing Co., Inc.
New York

Library of Congress Cataloging-in-Publication Data

Spence, William Perkins, 1925–
    Doors & entryways / William P. Spence.
        p. cm. -- (Building basics)
    Includes index.
    ISBN 0-8069-8111-3
    1. Doorways--Design and construction--Amateur's manuals. I. Title.
TH2278 .S64 2001
690'.8--dc21
                                                2001020775

Book Design: Judy Morgan
Series Editor: R. P. Neumann

1 3 5 7 9 10 8 6 4 2

Published by Sterling Publishing Company, Inc.
387 Park Avenue South, New York, N.Y. 10016
© 2001 by William P. Spence
Distributed in Canada by Sterling Publishing
c/o Canadian Manda Group, One Atlantic Avenue, Suite 105
Toronto, Ontario, Canada M6K 3E7
Distributed in Great Britain and Europe by Cassell PLC
Wellington House, 125 Strand, London WC2R 0BB, England
Distributed in Australia by Capricorn Link (Australia) Pty. Ltd.
P.O. Box 704, Windsor, NSW 2756 Australia
Printed in China
All rights reserved

Sterling ISBN 0-8069-8111-3

Contents

Selecting the Doors

Doors serve to provide access to the house and to its rooms. In addition they help ensure security for the space to which they allow access. However, doors serve other functions. Of great importance is their place in the exterior architecture of the building (**1-1**). They must be of a design that complements the style and represents the types of door used on the particular home.

The front entry door creates the initial impression a person gets when he approaches a house (**1-2**). From a distance the front entry is the focal point of the house and can make it an inviting and interesting building. The entry door with glass sidelights provides natural lighting into the foyer and creates a pleasant interior reception area (**1-3**). The selection of the entry-door system is a major decision.

Courtesy Weather Shield Manufacturing, Inc.

1-1 The entry door and the surrounding millwork are major factors in the architectural design of this house.

1-2 This front entrance gives a warm, friendly appearance.

1-3 This entry system has frosted, beveled glazing that provides natural light and privacy to the foyer.

FACTORS TO CONSIDER

In addition to the styling of the door and its relation to the architecture of the house, there are a number of factors to be considered as a decision is made on what door to use in each door opening. The choices are many and they deserve your time and energy investigating them before a final decision is made.

First consider the **materials.** Residential doors are typically wood, fiberglass, hardboard, steel or are clad with vinyl, aluminum, wood veneer, or high-pressure plastic laminates (**1-4**). Review Chapter 3. The **construction** of the door varies, and more expensive doors have better construction and higher-quality materials. The materials also affect the **cost.** If a door is in an area where it will get frequent use, a quality door is a good choice and a durable material should be considered. Consider whether an exterior door will require frequent maintenance, will warp and rot, or will be durable and resist the ravages of weather.

1-4 This is a fiberglass exterior door that can be stained the desired wood color and is energy efficient.

1-5 (Above) The doors form an integral part of the overall interior design and in some cases are the dominant element.

1-6 (Left) This panel door has an attractive yet simple design. It has a hardwood core and hardwood outer layers and has undergone a special prefinishing process to seal the wood surfaces.

As the shape each room is considered and the design of the interior space is thought out, the selection of the doors going into a room can become part of both the **interior design** and the architectural statement that you are trying to achieve (**1-5**). Some rooms with only interior doors may do fine with a rather simple door that is durable and needs little maintenance. Some doors may need to meet stricter fire codes (**1-6**).

As interior and exterior design are considered, the **colors** of the doors become a factor. Some doors can be stained various wood colors. Others are paint-grade doors that will hold a good interior or exterior enamel for many years.

Exterior doors available have various degrees of **energy efficiency.** Solid-core doors or doors with a polyurethane foam core are more efficient than uninsulated hollow-core doors. If the door has extensive glazing or is a glass patio door, the energy efficiency of the glazing becomes a major consideration (**1-7**).

Also consider the **hardware** to be used. Doors that are frequently used and exposed to the elements should have quality hinges and hardware that functions easily for a long time and resists corrosion and damage from the weather. The appearance of the hardware, especially on the front entrance, is a factor (**1-8**).

Courtesy Kolbe and Kolbe Millwork Co.

1-7 This wood-framed French patio-door unit has energy-efficient glass that reduces heat loss and gain through the glazing.

1-8 Good-quality hardware will withstand weathering and last for years. Inexpensive exterior hardware will corrode and fail in a few years.

In some cases **ventilation** through the door is needed to provide fresh air to a room. Some doors have movable glazing with screens. Another approach is to use a storm door that permits the glazing to be removed or opened to provide ventilation.

Study the **types of door** available such as bifold, bypass, accordion, and pocket doors. They open up an area where a wide opening is needed. Large closets are a typical example. Refer to Chapter 4.

Consider where the door is to be used. For example, a swinging door into a small half bath could be a disaster (**1-9**). Select a door that provides access yet privacy. Study **clearances** as you select door widths. Narrow doors are a bother and a few extra inches are worth the cost. Should the house be prepared for someone who is wheelchair-bound, door widths and interior clearances must be considered to make all areas accessible.

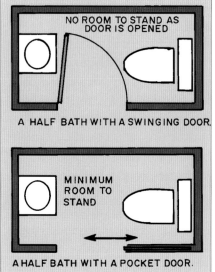

1-9
Be careful of the type of door you choose. Be certain it will provide adequate access and stay clear of all possible obstacles in the room.

You might consider, too, the **feel** of the door. Wood and hardboard doors have a warm, solid feel while steel doors feel hard and cold. Fiberglass doors have a solid, wood-like feeling.

Allowing your pets access to the outdoors or to certain areas of the house, such as the patio or basement, may be another factor to consider. See Chapter 8 for a discussion of pet access doors and their installation.

Finally consider the **cost.** Some prefer to put extra money into their doors to give a look of prominence, such as at the front entrance (**1-10**). If reducing expenses is a major goal, consider using interior doors with simpler designs, but be careful not to compromise quality for low-cost doors. Poor-quality doors will not function properly for very long.

1-10 Doors of significance to the decor and that make for pleasant living conditions may merit spending a little more.

PLANNING DOOR OPENINGS FOR THE WHEELCHAIR-BOUND

A single door opening should have a **minimum clear** opening of 32 inches (813mm). Notice in **1-11** that a 2'-8" (32-inch) door when hinged and with the doorstops on the jamb will not give the required clear opening. The 32-inch width is the minimum needed for a wheelchair to pass and leave room for a person's hands on the large wheels. When the door opening has depth (walls or cabinets on each side), a maximum depth of 24 inches (610mm) (**1-12**) is recommended. Door clearance requirements for various types of door are shown in **1-13**.

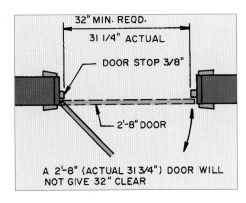

1-11 Be certain the door you choose will provide the required minimum opening.

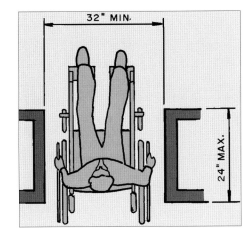

1-12 If the door enters a narrow area, it must be 32 inches (813mm) wide and the narrow area not longer than 24 inches.

1-13 Minimum door clearances for pocket, folding, and hinged doors.

Planning Door Locations

When planning to build a new house or start an extensive remodeling job, careful consideration of the location of the doors will help produce a floor plan that provides easy access to all parts of the house, privacy where wanted, and views of scenic exterior vistas.

Planning the **foyer** is important because it is the focal point of the house and one of the major entry points. It also can provide those entering with an impressive first appearance (**2-1**). In many houses the foyer is centrally located (**2-2**). It is large enough for several

Courtesy Therma-Tru Doors

2-1 These fiberglass double entry doors open up the foyer to the visitor and make a fine first impression.

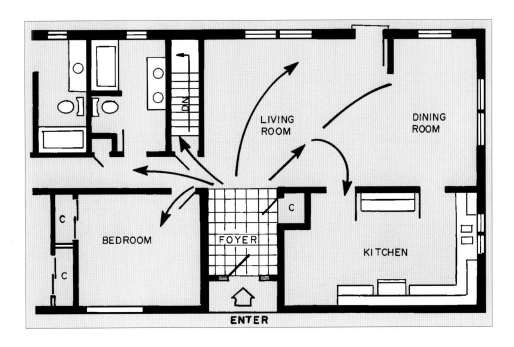

2-2 The foyer is the center of attention as guests enter and provides access to all parts of the house. A large, attractive floor area is an important design feature. Quality entrance doors and sidelights contribute to the overall success of the foyer design.

guests to enter and has a closet for hanging coats. The door must be at least 36 inches (914mm) wide. More elaborate entries have double doors (**2-3**) and even sidelights.

Some floor plans have the **stair** to the second floor centrally located near the front entry. If the stair is close by the front door (**2-4**), the door when open blocks the stair.

Courtesy Weather Shield Manufacturing Co.

2-3 These entryway double doors set the style for the passage into the foyer.

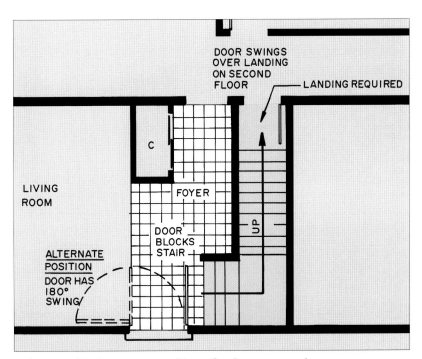

2-4 Poor planning creates problems for the entryway door.

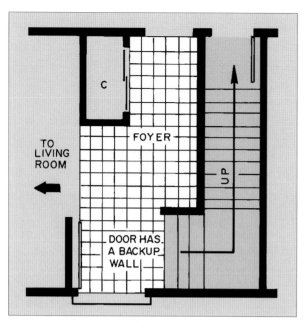

2-5 A small wall provides a backing for the door and also can create a pleasant arched opening into the living room.

Try to avoid letting doors block access to any part of the house. The door could swing on the left doorframe, but it would swing all the way back against the wall. Doors should open and stand against a wall. This could be corrected if a wall were built to frame in a small foyer (2-5). In 2-6 the stairs are located in the center of the house and the entry door lets traffic flow directly to them. In 2-7 notice that the open front door blocks the closet door and that they will hit if one is already open. This arrangement will not permit visitors to hang up their coats unless they have all moved well into the foyer and the entry door has been closed.

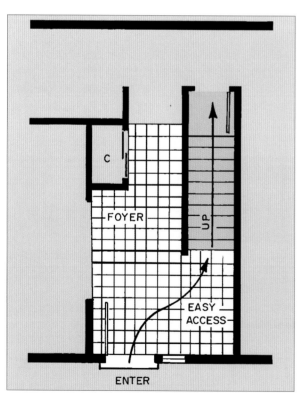

2-6 This stair is located near the center of the house, providing easy access to it from the foyer.

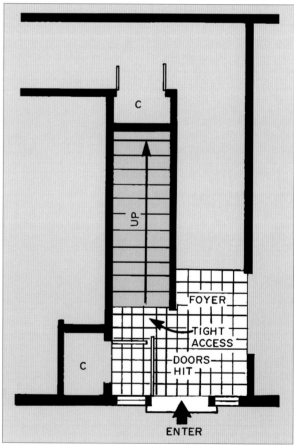

2-7 Here are some further door problems. The closet is blocked when the entry door is opened. Also the open door makes it difficult to use the stair.

When planning the **bathroom** be certain the door clears all the fixtures and has a wall or storage cabinet against which it will stand when open (**2-8** and **2-9**). Also place the door so anyone coming down the hall does not have to look straight in on the toilet. Place a nice vanity or storage wall to be the view. In **2-8** the toilet is clearly in view, while in **2-9** it is somewhat out of sight.

It is fairly easy to place the **bedroom** door so that privacy is provided for most of the room. This is usually accomplished by placing the entry door in one corner (**2-10**). Again, the door should open back against a wall. When planning the bedroom consider the door in relation to the windows. Establish their locations relative to each other so that a natural ventilation flow is allowed to occur.

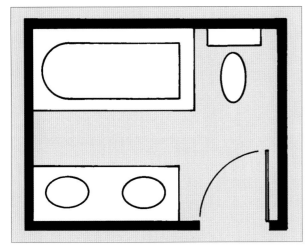

2-8 This small bathroom (minimum recommended size, with two lavatories) has the door opening against a wall that provides space for a person to enter.

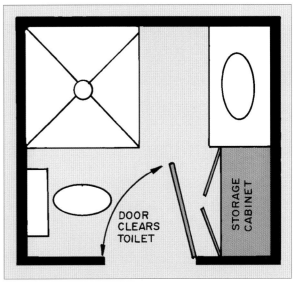

2-9 Here the door will open back against the storage cabinet. While acceptable, the cabinet cannot be opened until the bathroom door is closed. Be sure to check to see if the door clears the toilet.

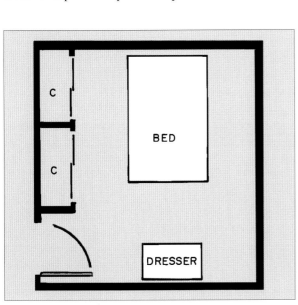

2-10 A good way to locate a door in a bedroom is to place it in a corner.

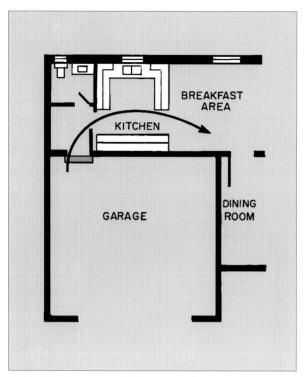

2-11 The location of this garage door into the house turns the kitchen into a hall that causes great inconvenience.

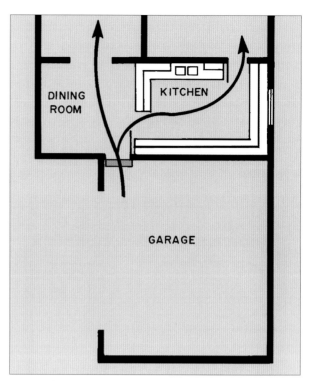

2-12 The location of this garage door into the house directs traffic through the dining room or through the kitchen. Both routes are very poor choices.

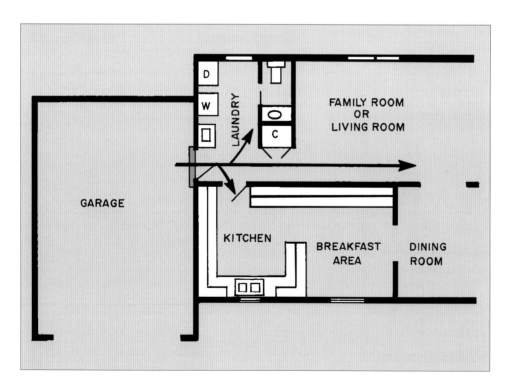

2-13 This garage-door entry into the house uses a small hall past the laundry door and kitchen door. It provides clear access to the kitchen and laundry room. It does make one side of the family room serve as a hall, but this does not bother most of the room.

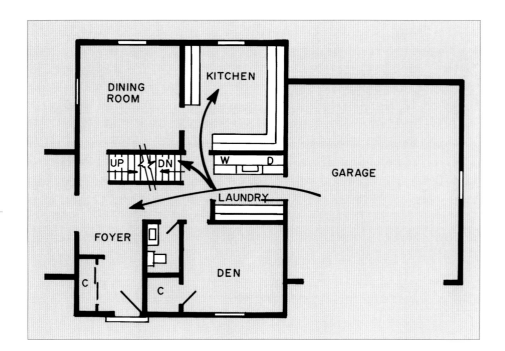

2-14 The garage-door entry in the house provides easy access to the first-floor rooms. It makes a hall out of the laundry, but this room is seldom occupied.

Doors into **kitchens** take considerable planning. If improperly placed, the kitchen (**2-11**) or some other room becomes a hall and the through traffic can be a bother (**2-12**). When planning the kitchen, try to locate the doors similar to those in **2-13** and **2-14**. The garage is located near the kitchen so it is easy to bring in the food purchases and remove the trash; so this can be a real planning problem. Do not make the garage-entrance door too small. Because large packages may need to come through it, make it at least 2'-8" (813mm) wide.

Generally **dining rooms** do not have entrances with doors. They will have framed openings of various sizes. However, if the dining room is to be enclosed, the door needs to be located so it opens against a wall and clears all furniture. It should not crowd the table or chairs (**2-15**).

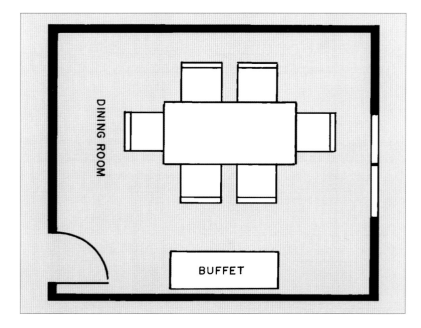

2-15 The door into a dining room should clear the furnishings and provide easy access to the table.

The **living room** may be located differently from house to house. Like the dining room, it will typically not have doors that can close it off from the rest of the home. Often the living room will be placed so that one outside wall faces a pleasant view (**2-16**). A patio or deck may extend out from this wall, and the living-room wall can be a long series of sliding glass doors or French doors (**2-17**). The living room may have a wall that has a sunroom on the other side so that glass doors here provide wide access, ventilation, and a view through the sunroom to the outside (**2-18**). The view through the sunroom reveals the pleasant plantings in the back acreage (**2-19**).

When planning a **laundry room**, decide what activities will take place there. Typically these will include storing clothes to be washed, using a washer and dryer, storing supplies, and ironing (**2-20**). The door should be wide enough so the washer and dryer can be moved into the room. Generally a 32-inch (812mm) clear opening is adequate. Space is needed so the door can remain open and not block the use of any of the appliances or access to the cabinets.

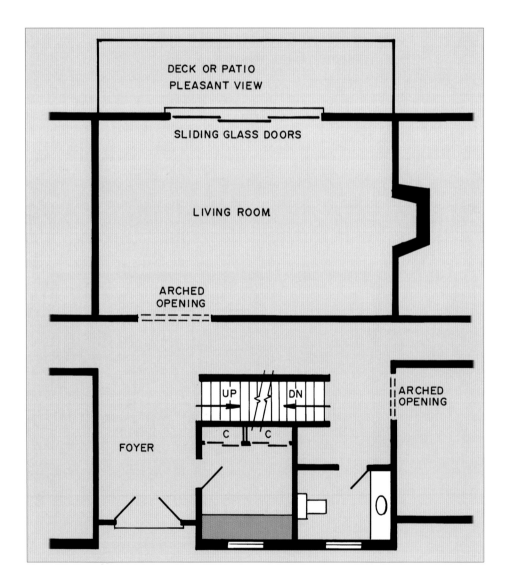

2-16 Doors can provide access to patios and decks as well as reveal a pleasant view.

DOORS & ENTRYWAYS

2-17 These sliding wood doors provide an extensive view of the scenery in the distance and provide access to the deck.

2-18 These vinyl-clad aluminum sliding-glass doors provide access from the living room into the sunroom.

2-19 The sunroom provides a sweeping view of the exterior scene.

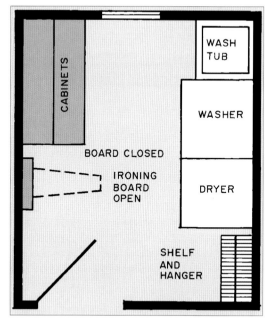

2-20 The laundry room contains several large appliances. The door must permit them to be moved in and out of the room. The door should clear all appliances, sinks, and ironing facilities.

There are many types of door used on **closets.** These include hinged, bypass sliding, and bifold. The closet opening size will be determined by the stock sizes of the type of door to be used. The door chosen should clear the furniture. For this reason bypass and bifold doors are frequently used (**2-21**).

If a **home workshop** is planned, it is often placed in the basement, although some designs work it into a large garage or even a separate small building in the yard. A 36-inch (914mm) door is needed for access for ordinary use. However, it is important to have a larger outside door. Machines, plywood panels, and completed projects are large and need a 5- or 6-foot (1525 or 1830mm) opening. Double doors are recommended (**2-22**).

2-21 (Above) Bifold doors are used on closets because they open to reveal a wide space while not extend into the room more than a few inches.

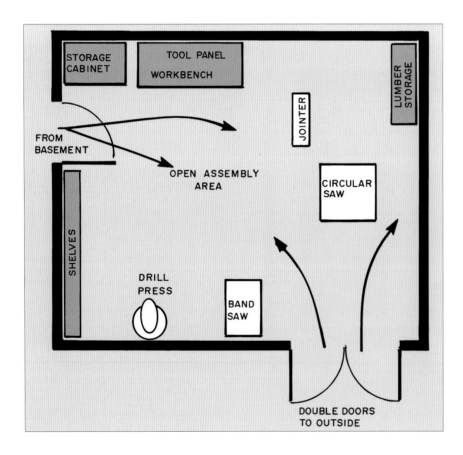

2-22 Large doors are needed when they lead into a home workshop.

BUILDING CODES

Building codes are established to protect the welfare, health, and safety of the community. They provide minimum requirements to be met by the design and construction of a building and the materials to be used. Typical examples relating to doors are given in **Table 2-1**. Specific requirements must be found by examining the local building code.

TABLE 2-1 TYPICAL BUILDING CODES RELATING TO DOORS & ENTRYWAYS*

Egress

Each dwelling should have a least one exit door providing direct access from the habitable areas of the dwelling without requiring travel through a garage.

All exterior doors should be operable from the side that exits to the outside and should be operable without the use of a key or special tool.

Exit doors should be side-hinged, at least 3 feet (914mm) in width, and 6'-8" (2032mm) high.

Exit doors on a stairway should open in the direction of travel.

Exterior Doors

Exterior doors must meet wind loads specified by the code.

Glass exterior doors should be tested by an independent laboratory and the results and name of the manufacturer be placed on each door. Tests are to be made according to the standards specified by the code.

Exterior glass doors on dwellings in hurricane-prone areas should provide protection according to code-specified standards.

Exterior glass doors should be anchored to the structural system of the building following code-specified methods.

Exterior glass doors should be anchored in accordance with the manufacturer's directions.

Mullions between exterior glass doors should be tested by an independent testing laboratory.

Landings

A landing or floor is required on each side of an exterior door. The floor or landing should not be more than 1½ inches (38mm) below the top of the threshold.

The width of any landing should be equal to or greater than the width of the door swinging over it, but should be at least 36 inches (914mm).

Doors from a Garage

Doors from a private garage directly into a bedroom are not permitted.

Doors from a private garage into a house should be 1⅜-inch solid wood or 1⅜-inch solid core or honeycomb-core steel doors or a door with a 20-minute or greater fire rating.

---

* Specific requirements must be found by examining the local building code.

Door Materials & Construction

The choice of materials used to build doors has greatly expanded over the years. Each material has merits as well as possible factors you may not like for a particular application. As doors are chosen, these factors must be considered so the best door for the situation can be selected. Also to be considered are appearance, durability, ease of finishing, and cost (3-1).

The method of construction used for the doors should also be considered. Strength, weight, ability to resist forced entry, and prospective life are important factors. Obviously the doors with the best construction will cost more. The following discussions address considerations and details for the commonly used materials and methods of door construction.

Courtesy Therma-Tru Doors

BOWING

When doors are exposed to the weather, moisture can destroy the finish or lead to deterioration, but it is the changes in temperature especially that can cause doors to bow slightly. This is caused by the expansion of the material when heated by the sun's rays. Fiberglass doors have the highest coefficient of expansion, steel is next, and wood has the lowest. As a door

3-1 This fiberglass entry system provides a durable door and sidelights. They can be finished by staining and sealing with a topcoat provided by the manufacturer to give the appearance of wood

They are typically heavier than those of other materials, and home owners like the solid feeling as they are opened that is indicative of quality.

Wood doors are easy to work because they can be planed on the edges and cut to length and width; scratches can be filled, sanded, and refinished, and holes can be easily bored for hardware.

Wood doors are available for use in all situations including entry systems and other exterior openings as well as interior doors and special units such as French and patio doors (3-4).

3-2 Solid-wood exterior doors provide the beauty of the real grain and can be stained with a wide range of wood colors.

3-3 Wood doors are available in several types of wood and can be finished in a range of wood tones. They can be planed and cut to fit.

bows, it may separate from being in contact with the weatherstripping—which could let air and water infiltrate. This is one reason designers like to provide some form of protection for exterior doors. A porch, small roof, or recess for the door into the house is a good way to protect a door. Refer to Chapter 9 for more details on methods of sheilding exterior doors.

DOORS MADE FROM WOOD & WOOD PRODUCTS

Wood doors are perhaps the most appealing of all the materials used, because of wood's natural grain and beauty. They can be stained to provide a wide array of wood tones and painted if a particular color is wanted. They are generally available in pine, fir, oak, and mahogany (3-2).

Wood doors are also available in a wide range of styles with a choice of panels, lights, and moldings. The more expensive wood doors are made using thick panels and wide stiles and rails (3-3).

3-4 Wood doors are widely used for exterior and interior applications, such as these sliding patio doors.

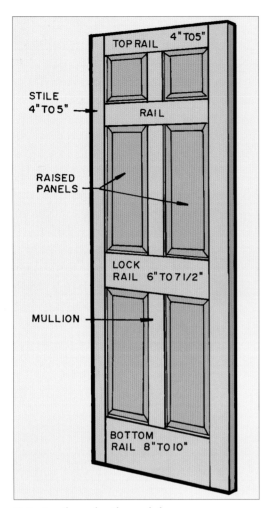

3-5 A stile-and-rail wood door.

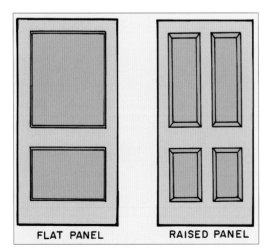

3-6 Panels in stile-and-rail doors may be raised or flat.

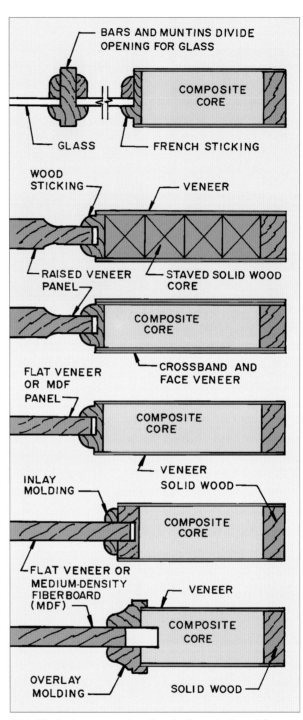

3-7 Typical construction details for raised and flat panels and for glazed stile-and-rail doors.

STILE-&-RAIL WOOD DOORS

Stile-and-rail wood doors have been the major type of construction for residential exterior and interior doors for many years, and they remain very popular. Typical construction of a stile-and-rail foor is shown in **3-5**. The name came from the use of substantial vertical stiles and horizontal rails. The interior of the door consists of panels set between the stiles, rails, and a central member called a mullion. The stiles are typically 4 to 5 inches (102 to 127mm) wide. The top rail is made the same width as the stiles, while the bottom rail is generally 8 to 10 inches (203 to 254mm) wide. The size and number of panels can vary as decided by the manufacturer. Refer back to **3-1**, **3-2**, and **3-3**. The panels may be raised or flat (**3-6** and **3-7**).

Stile-and-rail doors are available 1⅜ and 1¾ inch (35 and 44mm) thick. The 1¾-inch door is used for exterior installations. Some manufacturers make a 2¼-inch (57mm)-thick door. This is a more massive and impressive product.

The joints between the stiles and rails can vary depending upon the manufacturer, many using a dowel joint. The edges of the stiles are shaped to receive the panel. This is referred to as the sticking. The ends of the rails are shaped to fit over the sticking and are said to be coped (**3-8**). The panels are machined to fit into the grooves, and are left dry—not glued in—when the door is assembled. Since wood expands and contracts due to temperature changes, the panel must be free to move in the groove. If they are glued in place, they will eventually split.

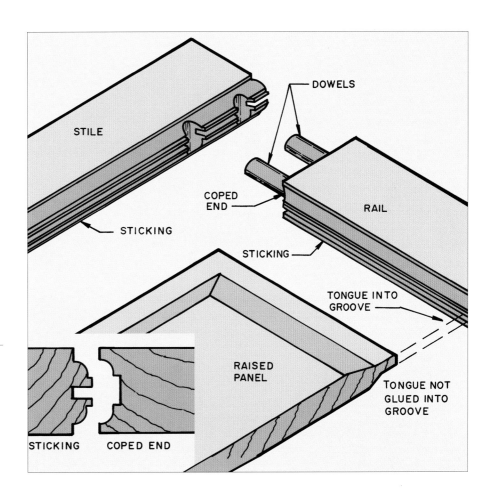

3-8 Stile-and-rail connections are often made by running the sticking up the stile and coping the end of the rail to fit over the sticking. Dowels are used to secure the joint.

STAIN-GRADE STILE-&-RAIL DOORS

Many stain-grade stile-and-rail doors available today do not use solid stiles and rails because of the expense of the wood that would be required in the thickness needed. A less expensive wood is used for the stiles and rails and only a veneer of the more attractive wood is bonded to the surface. Actually the stiles and rails can be made from smaller lengths of wood jointed with finger joints to produce the lengths needed (**3-9**). The natural wood veneer is glued over this, producing a "solid" wood door. This type of construction produces a quality door. Some doors bond the veneer to an exterior-grade fiberboard core.

Another construction technique for stiles, rails, and panels is the lamination of two pieces of wood—high-quality wood or wood to which veneer is then glued (**3-10**). For panels, this reduces the chance that they will warp or crack.

PAINT-GRADE WOOD STILE-&-RAIL DOORS

Doors that will be painted are often made with a low-cost wood, such as poplar, for both the rails and stiles and with medium-density fiberboard (MDF) for the panels. What is wanted in a paint-grade door is a smooth surface that will take interior enamels. Some low-cost paint-grade doors available have stiles and rails made with finger-jointed lumber and are not covered with a paint-grade veneer. The key to success is getting such a door with the joints so well made that they do not show through the paint.

WOOD FLUSH DOORS

Wood flush doors are available in three grades. The **premium grade** has the highest-quality materials and workmanship. The vertical edges have the best appearance and the face veneers are balanced and center-matched. The **custom grade** has normal-quality materials and workmanship. It is still a high-quality door. The **economy grade** uses the lowest-grade materials approved by standards and is the lowest priced of the three grades.

Flush doors have a smooth exterior skin and provide none of the decorative features found on stile-and-rail doors (**3-11**). The skin is bonded to and conceals the rails, stiles, or other members forming the structural framework. They are available with hollow and solid cores. The **hollow-core door** has a honeycomb core made of a fibrous material (**3-12**). Hollow-core

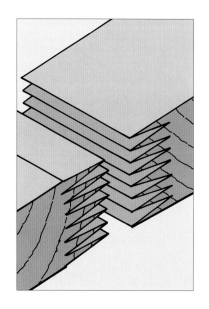

3-9 Stiles and rails that are covered with a quality wood veneer can be made from wood pieces joined with glued finger joints. The joints are actually stronger than the rest of the wood member.

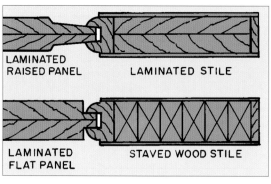

LAMINATED RAISED PANEL   LAMINATED STILE

LAMINATED FLAT PANEL   STAVED WOOD STILE

3-10 Some stile-and-rail wood doors are made with two-piece laminated stiles, rails, and panels.

doors are not fire rated and have poor sound-transmission properties. Moldings can be installed on the surface giving the appearance of panel construction. The skin may be wood crossband veneer or a high-pressure plastic laminate. The wood veneer is typically 2 or 3 ply and the plastic laminate 0.050 inch (1.3mm) thick. Wood veneers frequently used include mahogany, birch, oak, and walnut.

Solid-core flush doors may have a core of wood blocks glued together and framed with wood edge bands glued to the core (**3-13**). The skin is formed by bonding two or three layers of wood veneer or by using a high-pressure plastic laminate as the face veneer. Solid-core

3-11 Flush doors have the entire face covered with a quality wood veneer or a high-pressure plastic laminate. They may have a solid or hollow core.

doors are also available with particleboard and composite-lumber cores. They have a 1⅜-inch (34.9mm) wood edge bonded to the core (**3-14**). Flush fire-rated doors have a mineral core. The edge bonding meets special requirements, and the face has a crossband veneer bonded to the core and a high-pressure plastic laminate as the face veneer. Special designs are used to produce doors to reduce sound transmission, to block X rays, and even to be bullet resistant.

Industry standards for wood doors are available from the Window and Door Manufacturers Association, 1400 E. Touhy Ave., Suite 470, Des Plains, IL 60018-3337.

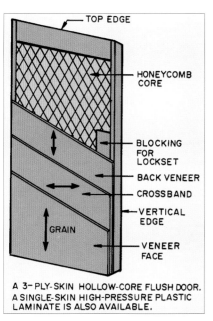

3-12 Typical construction details for hollow-core flush doors.

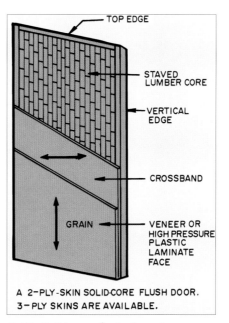

3-13 Solid-core flush doors have two or three veneers laminated over the wood core.

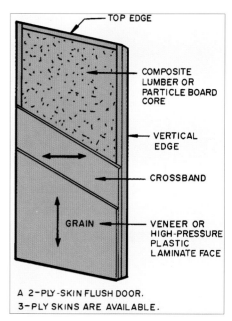

3-14 Solid-core doors are available with particleboard and composite lumber cores.

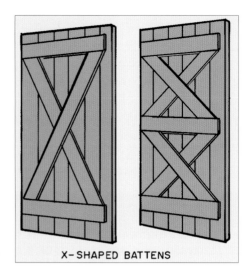

X-SHAPED BATTENS

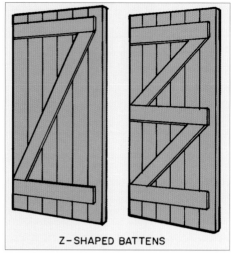

Z-SHAPED BATTENS

3-15 Batten wood doors provide a more rustic look.

BATTEN WOOD DOORS

Batten doors are constructed with a series of solid-wood vertical planks that are connected with boards mounted on the surface (**3-15**). These originally were found on barns and other storage buildings. Their roughness and uniqueness have contributed to current use in houses of ranch and rural home styles. They do seem to expand more than factory-made doors and are more difficult to keep flat and straight.

Key to success is to use quality kiln-dried lumber and a finish that completely seals out moisture. Interior doors can be made from ¾-inch (18mm) tongue and groove lumber. However, 1¼-inch (32mm) lumber is better. Exterior doors should be at least of 1½-inch (38mm) stock; however, thicker stock would be better (**3-16**). Battens on interior doors should be 1¼ inches thick and on exterior doors at least 1½ inches thick (**3-16**). Battens are typically 6 to 8 inches (152 to 203mm) wide and are secured with screws. Do not edge-glue the boards or battens to the stock, butl allow the wood to expand and contract, reducing the likelihood of the door's bowing.

FINISHING WOOD DOORS

When selecting major entrance-door systems, consider selecting one of the finishing systems offered by the manufacturer. The finish will be applied under controlled conditions as the door is made. The finish will be high-quality and free

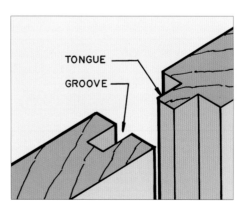

TONGUE

GROOVE

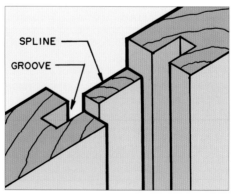

SPLINE

GROOVE

3-16 The boards forming the door can be joined using tongue-and-groove stock or joined on the edges with a spline.

of blemishes. If the system is finished on the site, conditions for a quality job are limited by the possibility of dust, moisture, and less-than-desirable application techniques. When you spend several thousand dollars for an entry-door system, a quality finish is expected.

Interior doors can also be factory finished but they can be site finished more easily than exterior doors because they are inside the building. A quality job requires a painting crew that will carefully sand each door, remove the dust at the entranceway as well as inside the house. The use of quality application tools is important. It is hard to do a better job than the factory finish.

Exterior doors can be finished using an exterior paint. The paint dealer can help select a primer and topcoat that will withstand exposure to the weather. The color used is generally the same as is used on the exterior trim. However, some give the main entrance door more prominence by painting it a strong color. The entrance can also be embellished with the addition of detailed entrance trim made with quality moldings and accent pieces (3-17).

The natural wood color is one choice for interior and exterior doors. Natural wood could be covered with a sealing topcoat to protect it from moisture. Many times the door is stained to

Courtesy Style-Mark, Inc.

3-17 Attention can be focused on the main entrance by painting the door a bright color and embellishing the entryway with detailed architectural entrance trim. This trim was molded from high-density urethane.

enhance the appearance and give emphasis to the grain (3-18). A semi-transparent oil stain is often used. The topcoat is often two or more coats of UV-inhibiting polyurethane.

Interior doors may also be painted or stained and finished with an overcoat. The paint used will most often be an interior latex enamel. It is available in a range of colors and several degrees of gloss. Stained interior doors can use a lacquer or varnish topcoat because they are not exposed to the weather.

Regardless of the finish used, the edges of the door must be sealed to keep moisture from penetrating and possibly causing swelling.

Courtesy Simpson Door Company

3-18 Wood doors can be stained for color and to enhance the grain.

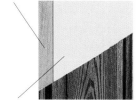

WOOD EDGE FOR MOUNTING
HANDSET HARDWARE

POLYURETHANE FOAM CORE
COVERED WITH FIBERGLASS
SKIN PROVIDES FIVE TIMES
THE R-VALUE OF WOOD

3-19 Fiberglass doors
have a wide wood edge to
carry the lock and hinges,
and a polyurethane foam
core, covered with
fiberglass skin.

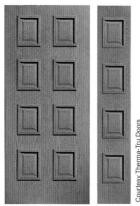

Courtesy Therma-Tru Doors

3-20 This grained,
stained fiberglass door
appears much the same
as a wood door.

FIBERGLASS DOORS

Fiberglass doors consist of a frame of wood stiles
and rails with a polyurethane foam core. The
fiberglass skin is laminated over this assembly
(**3-19**). This is a well-insulated door providing
about five times the insulating value of a typical
wood door.

The fiberglass skin has a wood grain worked
into it and, when finished to a wood color, it
looks like a solid-wood door (**3-20**).

Manufacturers claim that their fiberglass
doors will not crack, warp, rot, or split. Most
offer a long warranty. Some even offer a lifetime
limited warranty.

Some fiberglass doors have the skin flush with
the stiles (**3-21**). The edge of the skin can be seen
when the door is open, but this is usually not
noticeable. Other styles set the edge of the skin
in a notch on the edge of the stile. This leaves a
bit of wood showing and makes it possible to
plane a little off the edge to fit the door. Of
course you should stop planing before you reach
the edge of the fiberglass. When the door is
closed, the exposed wood on the edge is visible
but not very noticeable. Actually it appears as if
there were a wider distance between the door
and the jamb than actually exists. The bottom
rail of exterior doors should be a rot-resistant
wood and have some type of plastic or rubber
finished edge to stop air and water leakage and
protect the skin and core (**3-22**).

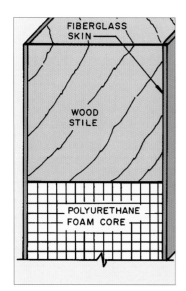

FIBERGLASS
SKIN

WOOD
STILE

POLYURETHANE
FOAM CORE

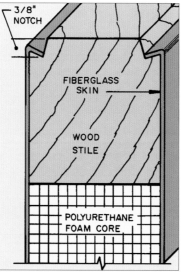

3/8"
NOTCH

FIBERGLASS
SKIN

WOOD
STILE

POLYURETHANE
FOAM CORE

Courtesy Therma-Tru Doors

3-21 When fiberglass doors are made, there are several ways that
the manufacturerer may end the skin at the edge of the door.

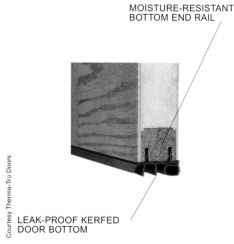

MOISTURE-RESISTANT
BOTTOM END RAIL

LEAK-PROOF KERFED
DOOR BOTTOM

3-22 It is important that the bottom
edge of the door have a very good
door-bottom seal and that it be set
in a moisture-resistant bottom rail.

Fiberglass doors can have lights of many sizes and shapes. The glass is glazed into the door as it is being made (**3-23**). The polyurethane foam bonds to the glass, forming a water-tight seal.

Fiberglass fire doors do not have lights. They are made with solid-fiber fire-barrier layers with a polyurethane core between. A fiberglass skin is laid on each side.

FINISHING
A FIBERGLASS DOOR

The composition of the fiberglass skin varies some, depending upon the manufacturer. This affects how the door is finished.

3-23 Fiberglass doors can have glazing in a wide range of sizes and designs.

The manufacturers of fiberglass doors offer a range of stain colors (**3-24**). These can be varied on the site by the amount of stain applied. This range of color permits a wide range of tones, allowing the door to match the desired décor. The manufacturer also supplies the recommended topcoat and finishing instructions (**3-25**).

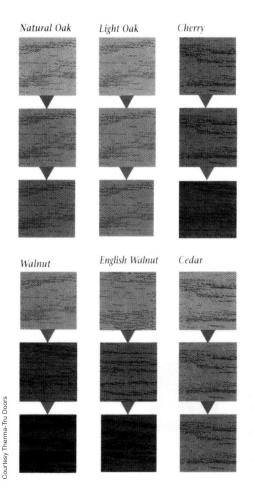

3-24 One fiberglass door manufacturer offers this wide range of stain colors.

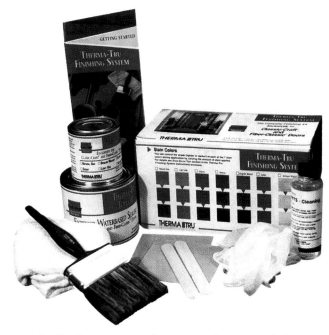

3-25 The finishing system of one manufacturer includes stain, mineral spirits, clear water-based topcoat, proper brush, gloves, mixing sticks, color samples, and complete instructions.

Sometimes the topcoat deteriorates and peals (**3-26**). This is especially true if the manufacturer-recommended topcoat is not used. It can be cleaned and refinished. Begin by wiping the surface with mineral spirits to remove the weathered topcoat. Do not sand, because this will remove the grain indentions. The topcoat should be renewed every 3 to 5 years or when the gloss begins to fade. If this is done, it is not usually necessary to restain the door.

HARDBOARD DOORS

Hardboard is a reconstituted-wood material manufactured of wood fibers compressed under heat and pressure into sheets, panels, and products such as doors.

Hardboard door skins are molded from this material and are available in a range of designs such as the one in **3-27** that has the molded fiberboard skin resembling a stile-and-rail door.

Hardboard doors may have a **solid core** over which the molded hardboard skin is bonded (**3-28**). These are heavy doors and usually used for entry doors. Since they have good sound-blocking properties, hardboard doors are also used as interior doors where sound blocking is important. **Hollow-core hardboard** doors have a molded hardboard skin bonded to a wood frame of stiles and rails. The core is made of corrugated cardboard (**3-28**). These are used as interior doors. They are lighter and cost less.

3-26 If the wrong topcoat is used or the correct topcoat is not renewed when it loses the gloss, it could deteriorate and peel.

STEEL DOORS

Steel doors are constructed by bonding a steel skin over a wood stile-and-rail frame (**3-29**). The hollow core is filled with polyurethane or polystyrene. The door with a polyurethane-formed core will have a much higher insulation value than one with polystyrene. These doors are shipped with a factory-applied primer ready for painting. Some have a rust-inhibiting plating over the bare metal before it is primed.

The steel skin has panels stamped into it so it resembles a wood-panel stile-and-rail door (3-30). Some types have a simulated wood-grain texture rolled into the steel skin. Steel-skin doors are available with a PVC vinyl layer bonded over the steel skin forming the visible surface. This provides a more realistic wood-grain pattern and can be finished with manufacturer-recommended stains and a clear UV-inhibiting topcoat. Wood-color stains are widely used with this product.

3-27 This hardboard door has molded skins bonded to a solid core. This produces a heavy, sound-deadening door.

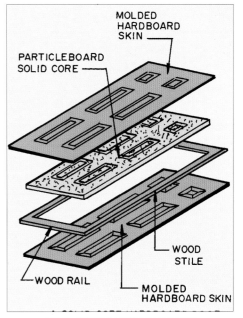

MOLDED HARDBOARD SKIN

CORRUGATED CARDBOARD HONEYCOMB CORE

PARTICLEBOARD SOLID CORE

MOLDED HARDBOARD SKIN

WOOD STILE

WOOD STILE

MOLDED HARDBOARD SKIN

WOOD RAIL

WOOD RAIL

MOLDED HARDBOARD SKIN

HOLLOW-CORE HARDBOARD DOOR

SOLID-CORE HARDBOARD DOOR

3-28 Hardboard skins are bonded to a frame of wood stiles and rails. Hollow core doors have a core of corrugated cardboard that results in a lightweight door. Solid-core doors have a particleboard core.

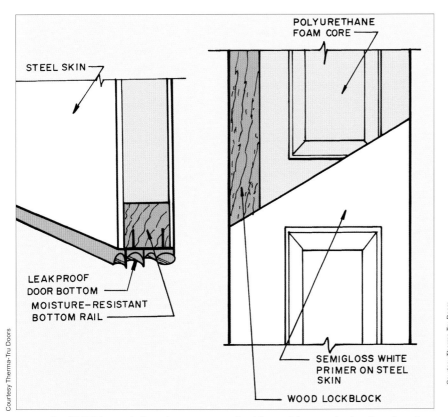

POLYURETHANE FOAM CORE

STEEL SKIN

LEAKPROOF DOOR BOTTOM

MOISTURE–RESISTANT BOTTOM RAIL

SEMIGLOSS WHITE PRIMER ON STEEL SKIN

WOOD LOCKBLOCK

Courtesy Therma-Tru Doors

3-29 (Left) This steel door is constructed with a wide wood edge band and a core filled with polyurethane foam that provides excellent insulation properties. The steel skin is laid over this core.

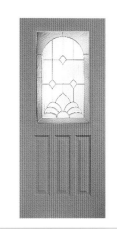

Courtesy Therma-Tru Doors

3-30 (Above) This steel door has panels resembling a wood door along with a glazed opening.

Quality steel doors will have an electro-galvanized steel skin that is designed to provide protection against rust. Industry standards indicate that the steel skin can be 16, 18, 20, or 24 gauge. The smaller the gauge number, the thicker the metal. For example, a 24-gauge skin is approximately 0.0250 inch (0.63mm) thick while a 16-gauge skin is 0.0625 inch (1.58mm) thick. The 16-gauge skin is a little more than twice as thick as the 24-gauge skin. Most residential doors are 20- or 24-gauge steel. The skin is factory primed and ready for painting. The foam core provides insulation value about five times greater than wood. On exterior doors the bottom rail should be a rot-resistant

3-31 This steel skin of this door stopped flush with the bottom; the bottom wood rail was not pressure-treated wood, so it rotted.

wood and have a moisture-resistant door bottom to reduce leakage and the possibility of rusting. Refer to **3-22**.

Doors that simply end the steel skin at the bottom will eventually rust if they are used as exterior doors. If the wood bottom rail is not made of pressure-treated wood, it will rot (**3-31**). The door should have a wood block installed in the core where the locks or a wide stile will be installed.

While steel doors are often installed in the same wood frames that are used for wood and fiberglass doors, some manufacturers offer a variety of vinyl and steel frames.

Steel doors that do not have wood stiles and rails should be made with a thermal break to separate the interior and exterior skins. Since metal is a good conductor of heat and cold, doors without a thermal break will move unwanted heat or cold to the interior of the house. Some typical construction details are shown in **3-32**. These show some ways that thermal breaks are provided. If there is no thermal break, the interior edge of the door may become covered with frost on the inside of the house because moisture-laden interior air will condense and freeze on it. Some doors with wood stiles and rails let the wood extend beyond the skin a little; this permits a little planing of the edge. Refer to **3-32**.

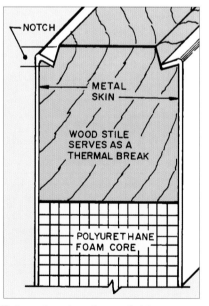

3-32 To provide the most energy-efficient situation the steel skins must be separated by a thermal break.

Steel doors are widely used as fire doors and can provide an attractive appearance (**3-33**). Hollow-metal fire doors typically have at least a 20-gauge skin. A fire rating for residential doors is typically 20 minutes. Consult the local code for specific requirements. The door manufacturer will have the fire ratings on each door.

Steel doors also provide protection against unlawful entry. They are strong and resist damage from blows that would break a wood—and possibly a fiberglass—door. Steel doors that have a steel frame running around the perimeter of the door will provide even better security. However, they do not have a thermal break.

Steel doors are available with internal blinds sealed between two panes of safety-tempered glass (**3-34**). Another type has a glazed window that lets the lower sash move vertically like a hung window, exposing a screened opening that provides ventilation.

Steel doors are available in a range of prices. The lower-cost doors are made of lighter-gauge metal. These will dent rather easily. Dents can be repaired by sanding the surface down to bare metal and filling the dent with auto-body filler just like that used on automobile dents. It can be sanded and refinished and the dent will be gone. Some steel doors do not permit the stile to be mortised (recessed) to set the hinge in flush. Some have mortises cut all the way across the stile so that a hinge is flush and the door can be hung for left-hand or right-hand installation. The edge of the hinge is visible on the inside of the door.

Courtesy Therma-Tru Doors

3-33 These steel fire-rated doors have the same attractive appearance as other doors. Those in this illustration have a 90-minute rating.

Courtesy Therma-Tru Doors

3-34 This type of steel door has a double-glazed light with venetian-type blinds between glazing.

ALUMINUM- & VINYL-CLAD DOORS

Aluminum- and vinyl-clad doors are manufactured much like steel and fiberglass doors. The cladding is bonded to the stiles and rails, wrapped around the edges of the door, and set into the stile or set into a dado or rabbet cut into the stile. The vinyl-clad door will not dent like the aluminum door and does not corrode as aluminum does under certain conditions. Both are available in several colors and provide long protection against the elements. They are available as prehung units that include the door, jamb, and hinges and are weatherstripped. This provides an air- and water-tight unit that is easy to install (**3-35**).

FIRE DOORS

Building codes specify the requirements for fire doors in residential construction. The **fire rating** of the door is the number of minutes a door will withstand a fire before failing. Codes usually require a 20-minute fire door between the garage and the house. This is typically a 1¾-inch (44mm)-thick solid-wood door, 1⅜-inch (35mm)-thick fiberglass or honeycomb-core steel door (refer to **3-33**), or any other door having a 20-minute fire rating (**3-36**). For example, many solid-core flush doors have a 20-minute fire rating. Doors are available that have 45-, 60-, and 90-minute ratings but the core material, skin, and construction are different. Steel, fiberglass, solid-wood, and composite doors also have a range of fire ratings, some as long as 3 hours. Actual ratings are available from the manufacturer.

Glazing and **louvers** in a fire door influence the fire rating and are controlled by codes. The doorframe must also have a fire rating. For use

3-35 These wood-framed vinyl-clad French doors have a durable exterior skin that weathers well.

3-36 Typical steel fire doors. These are available with 20-, 45-, and 90-minute fire ratings. The 20-minute door is typically used between the garage and house. The glazed door has a 10 × 10-inch window made of ¼-inch wire-mesh glass.

on fire doors between the garage and house, this is usually 20 minutes.

The fire door should be purchased pre-hung in a manufacturer-certified fire-related frame. The fire door should not be cut, trimmed, or drilled on the site; this could reduce the integrity of the door and reduce the fire rating. Codes also specify the hardware and control any laminated overlays.

DOORFRAMES

In residential construction the interior and exterior doorframes used are generally wood (3-37). These may have a solid one-piece jamb (3-38). Some doorframes are

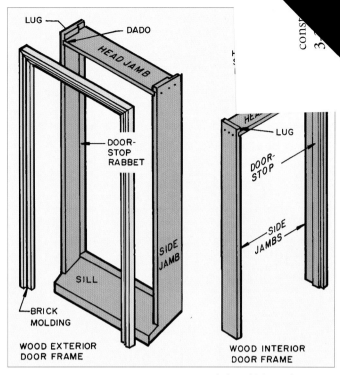

3-37 (Above) Typical interior and exterior wood doorframes.

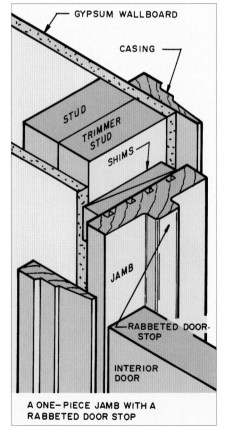

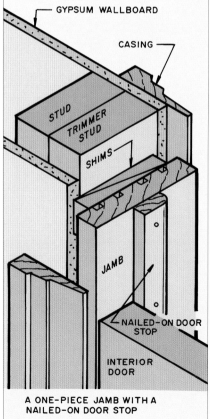

3-38 Single-piece doorframes may have the doorstop machined as part of the jamb or have a nailed-on doorstop.

...tructed with a split jamb, as shown in ...39. The type of frame that is selected changes the way the frame is installed, but the result is the same. Vinyl doorframes are used with vinyl doors such as the frame for the vinyl sliding patio doors in **3-40**. Aluminum and steel doorframes are available from some manufacturers. They are generally used on doors in commercial buildings, however.

Some residential-door manufacturers clad their wood frames with vinyl (**3-41**) or a hard wood veneer, such as oak. The vinyl-clad frames are very durable and resist the damages of weathering. The wood-veneer frames can be stained and finished with a topcoat.

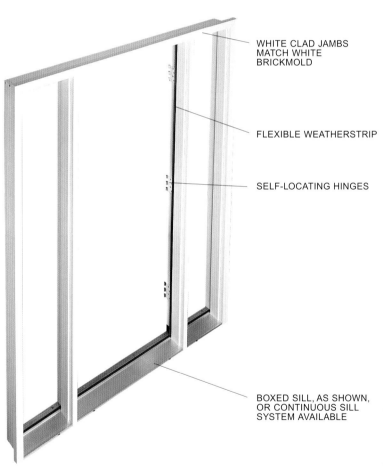

3-40 These vinyl doorframes and patio doors have multiple chambers that provide an energy-efficient installation.

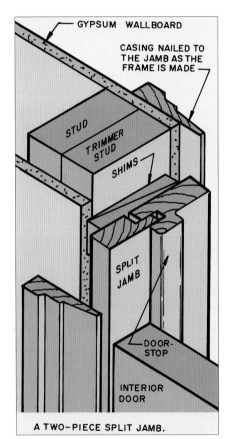

GYPSUM WALLBOARD

CASING NAILED TO THE JAMB AS THE FRAME IS MADE

STUD

TRIMMER STUD

SHIMS

SPLIT JAMB

DOOR-STOP

INTERIOR DOOR

A TWO-PIECE SPLIT JAMB.

3-39 A split-jamb doorframe has the jamb in two pieces. Each has the casing nailed to it and is installed from opposite sides of the door.

WHITE CLAD JAMBS MATCH WHITE BRICKMOLD

FLEXIBLE WEATHERSTRIP

SELF-LOCATING HINGES

BOXED SILL, AS SHOWN, OR CONTINUOUS SILL SYSTEM AVAILABLE

3-41 This is a wood doorframe that is clad with a durable vinyl, providing a durable, maintenance-free surface.

Typical doorframes for double doors and doors with sidelights are shown in **3-42**.

The doorframe used for a fire door must have a fire-rating that is equal to or exceeds that of the door. There are wood frames available rated at 20 minutes. Steel frames have a much better fire rating. The actual fire rating for a particular doorframe is available from the manufacturer.

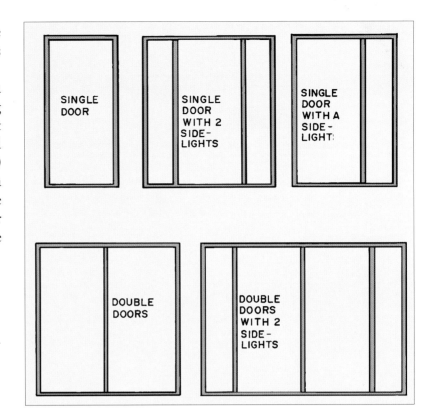

3-42 Doorframes for double doors and doors with sidelights are available from the door manufacturer.

CHAPTER 4

Types of Residential Door

Exterior and interior doors are available in a wide range of sizes, materials, and designs. They also vary considerably in cost, durability, energy efficiency, and sound-blocking properties. Visit a building supply-dealer to get an idea of what is available and write to the door manufacturers for their catalogs. The catalogs give details of doors and also discuss the materials available and the finishes that can be used. Chapter 3 gives details about the materials and how doors are constructed. This information is vital as a part of the door-selection process.

4-1 A few of the many designs and styles of exterior hinged door that are available.

Courtesy Therma-Tru Doors

TABLE 4-1 COMMON SIZES OF EXTERIOR HINGED DOORS & SIDELIGHTS

Exterior doors	
Thickness	1⅜", 1¾"
Height	6'-8", 7'-0"
Width	2'-6", 2'-8", 3'-0"
Sidelights	
Thickness	1⅜"
Height	6'-8½"
Width	0'-10", 1'-0", 1'-2", 1'-3", 1'-4", 1'-6"

TABLE 4-2 STOCK SIZES OF FLUSH DOORS

Hollow-core doors	
Thickness	1⅜", 1¾"
Height	6'-8", 7'-0", 8'-0", 10'-0"
Width	1'-6", 1'-8", 2'-0", 2'-4" 2'-6", 2'-8", 3'-0"
Solid-core doors	
Thickness	1⅜", 1¾", 2¼"
Height	6'-8", 7'-0"
Width	2'-4", 2'-6", 2'-8", 3'-0", 3'-4", 3'-6"

EXTERIOR HINGED DOORS

Exterior hinged doors are available in a wide variety of styles. They range from a simple flush door through many-panel designs and an extensive array of glazed units. Those in **4-1** are just a few of the many types available. They have sidelights designed to complement the door design. Exterior doors are usually 1¾ inches (44mm) thick. However, some companies make 1⅜-inch (35mm)-thick exterior doors. Common stock sizes are in **Table 4-1**. The materials and construction are discussed in Chapter 3.

Flush doors are used on interior and exterior openings. Commonly available sizes may be seen in **Table 4-2**.

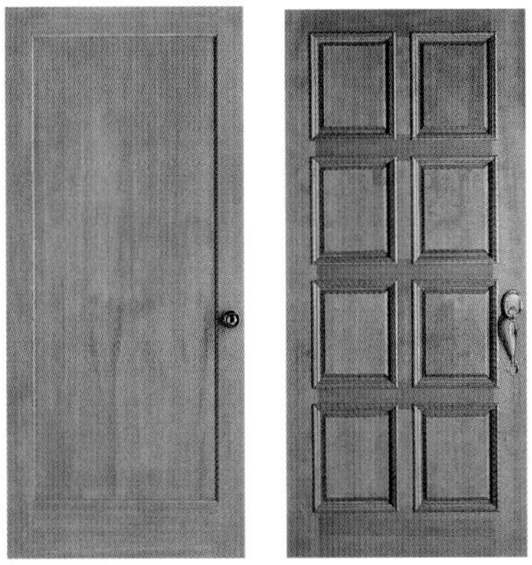

INTERIOR HINGED DOORS

Paneled interior hinged doors may have a flat or raised panel (**4-2**). Flush doors are also widely used on interior door openings (**4-3**). They may have a skin of wood veneer, plastic laminate, or hard board. Louvered doors are available for

Courtesy Simpson Door Company

4-2 These are flat- and raised-panel stile-and-rail interior doors. Many designs are available.

4-3 Flush doors are widely used on interior door openings.

TABLE 4-3 COMMON INTERIOR HINGED-DOOR SIZES

Thickness	1⅜"
Height	6'-6", 6'-8", 7'-0"
Width	1'-0", 1'-4", 1'-6", 1'-8", 2'-0", 2'-4", 2'-6", 2'-8" 3'-0"

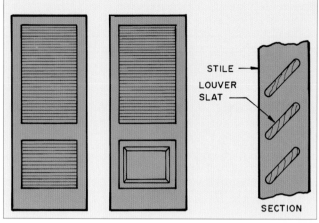

4-4 Interior louvered doors have wood stiles and rails. Wood slats are mortised into the stiles, forming the louver panel.

spaces, such as closets, where ventilation is needed (4-4). Some typical designs available for paneled interior doors are shown in 4-5; other styles are also available. Common stock sizes are given in **Table 4-3**. Refer to **Table 4-2** for flush door sizes.

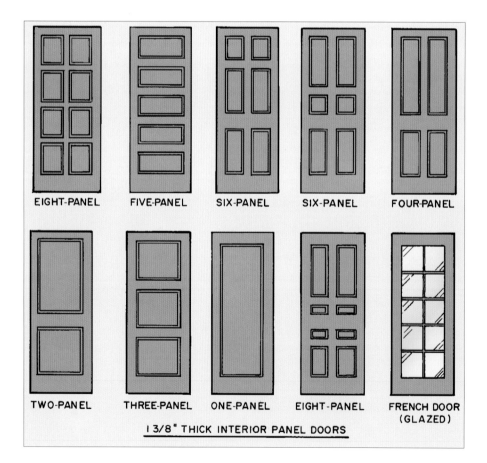

4-5 These are some typical panel designs for interior doors. Other designs are available from various manufacturers.

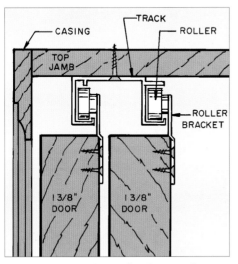

4-6 Bypass sliding doors open over each other, exposing half of the closet opening.

BYPASS DOORS

Sliding **bypass doors** move horizontally and allow only half of the closet to open at a time (**4-6**). They run on nylon wheels in a metal track that is screwed to the top jamb (**4-7** and **4-8**). The doors used are the lighter-weight 1⅜-inch interior doors. Typical installations can use two, three, or four doors (**4-9**). Be certain that the doors you have selected will be of a thickness that allows them to slide by each other using the hardware purchased.

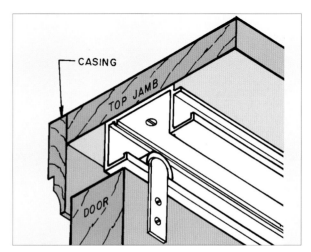

4-7 Bypass sliding doors run on a metal track attached to the head jamb of the doorframe. Rollers are attached to the top of the doors.

4-8 Typical hardware for the installation of two bypass doors. Be certain the hardware will handle the thickness of the doors to be used.

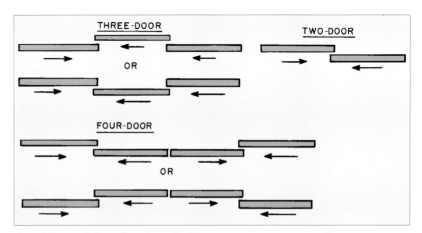

4-9 Bypass sliding door installations can use two or more doors.

TABLE 4-4 COMMON FRENCH-DOOR SIZES

Thickness	1⅜", 1¾"
Height	6'-8"
Width	2'-0", 2'-6", 2'-8", 3'-0"

FRENCH DOORS

French doors are used for exterior and interior installations (**4-10** and **4-11**). They are fully glazed and are available with a number of different sized and proportioned lights (**4-12**). The stiles and top rail are usually 4½ to 5 inches (114 to 127mm) wide and the bottom rail is usually at least 8 inches (203mm). Commonly available sizes are shown in **Table 4-4**.

PATIO DOORS

Patio doors are use to provide access to decks and patios and provide a large expanse of glass so the exterior scene can be viewed. They are available in wood, steel, or vinyl as well as wood clad with aluminum or vinyl. **Hinged patio doors** swing inward (**4-13**) and may consist of several doors. Some have two swinging doors while others have only one that swings (**4-14**). Sliding patio doors have one large moving panel that opens a large area (**4-15**). They are available in two- and four-door units (**4-16**). Typical sizes available are in **Table 4-5**.

4-10 French doors are installed in pairs and usually have many small glass panes. These are interior doors that provide a view into a den.

Courtesy Simpson Door Company

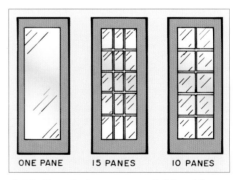

4-12 French doors are available with a number of glazing choices. They are used on interior and exterior openings.

ONE PANE   15 PANES   10 PANES

4-11 These are in-swinging French doors leading to a garden. Clear, beveled, and obscure glazing are available.

Courtesy Simpson Door Company

4-13 This aluminum-clad hinged patio door provides a wide view of the deck and surrounding area.

TABLE 4-5 COMMON PATIO-DOOR SIZES

Hinged doors	
Thickness	1¾"
Height	6'-7½"
Width	4'-11", 5'-11", 7'-11", 8'-11"

Sliding patio doors	
Thickness	1¾"
Height	6'-7½"
Width	4'-11", 5'-11", 7'-11", 9'-9", 11'-9", 15'-9"

4-15 This solid-vinyl sliding patio door has double-strength tempered glass and multiple barriers against air infiltration.

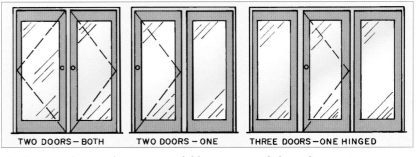

TWO DOORS—BOTH TWO DOORS—ONE THREE DOORS—ONE HINGED

4-14 Hinged patio doors are available in two- and three-door units with one or two swinging doors.

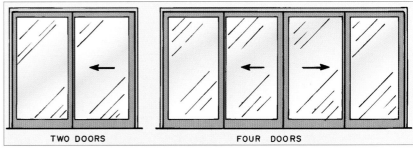

TWO DOORS FOUR DOORS

4-16 Sliding patio doors are available in two- and four-door units with one or two sliding doors.

TYPES OF RESIDENTIAL DOOR   43

TABLE 4-6 COMMON BIFOLD DOOR SIZES

Thickness	1⅜", 1¾"
Height	6'-6"
Widths	0'-8", 0'-9", 1'-0", 1'-3" 1'-4", 1'-6"

4-17 Bifold doors are a popular choice for closets because they open the entire area but do not extend out into the room very far.

BIFOLD DOORS

Bifold doors are typically sold in sets of two or four panels. They are most often used on closets because, when open, the entire area is exposed (**4-17**). Shown in **4-18** are standard layouts for two and four door openings and installations up to eight doors. Floor-mounted brackets are installed between every four doors. Commonly available door designs are in **4-19**. Common sizes may be seen in **Table 4-6**. The rails and stiles are usually narrower than those on hinged doors used on openings into rooms. They are connected with hinges, and the door next to the side jamb swings on a pivot made for this type of installation (**4-20**). The pivot at the floor can be adjusted by turning the nut on the threaded pin. This permits the door to be raised enough to clear the carpet (**4-21**).

The second door on a bifold installation has a pin in the top on the outside stile. This pin runs in the header track on the top jamb, guiding the door as it pivots on the hinges connecting it to the first door (**4-22**).

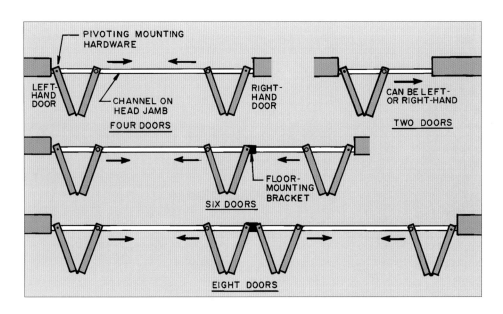

4-18 Bifold doors are installed with two-, four-, six-, and eight-door arrangements.

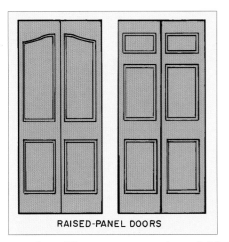

RAISED-PANEL DOORS

RAISED-PANEL DOORS

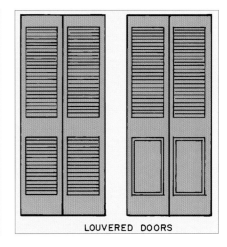

LOUVERED DOORS

4-19 There are commonly available bifold door designs.

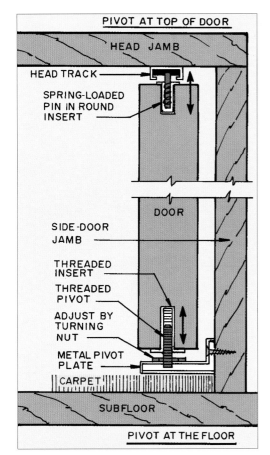

PIVOT AT TOP OF DOOR

HEAD JAMB

HEAD TRACK

SPRING-LOADED PIN IN ROUND INSERT

DOOR

SIDE-DOOR JAMB

THREADED INSERT

THREADED PIVOT

ADJUST BY TURNING NUT

METAL PIVOT PLATE

CARPET

SUBFLOOR

PIVOT AT THE FLOOR

4-20 Bifold doors swing on a pivot at the floor on the edge of the door next to the side jamb. The top of the door has a pin that fits into a metal insert in the channel.

4-21 Adjust the door pivot at the floor until the door clears the carpet as it swings open.

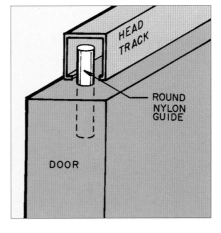

HEAD TRACK

ROUND NYLON GUIDE

DOOR

4-22 A pin is inserted in the top edge of the second door. It slides in the channel, guiding the door as it opens and closes.

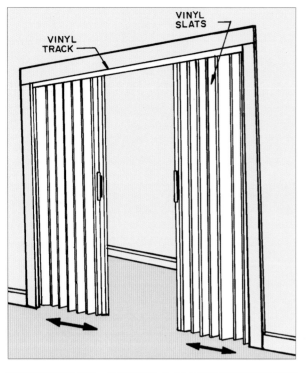

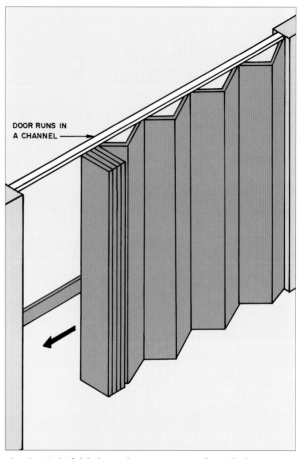

4-23 One type of multifold door has vinyl slats joined on the long edges with tape.

4-24 Multifold doors have a series of small door panels or narrow slats that are joined on the long edges. They unfold as they are pulled along a track that is mounted in the ceiling or along the head jamb of the door opening.

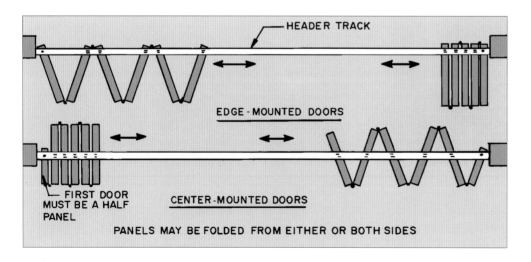

4-25 Multifold doors may be edge or center mounted on the overhead track.

MULTIFOLD DOORS

Multifold doors are much like bifold doors except they are made up of more panels. Some are very narrow and range from 4 to 5 inches (102 to 127mm). These tend to be single-thickness vinyl panels bound on the long edge with a vinyl tape (4-23). They run on a header track mounted on the head jamb of the door opening. Another type uses narrow wood panels typically 6 to 8 inches (152 to 203mm) wide (4-24). These may be edge-mounted or center-mounted, as shown in 4-25. They are mounted on a header track on the head jamb and sometimes will have a guide on the floor, recessed or surface-mounted, to make for smoother operation and eliminate door sway (4-26).

Large, multifold panel doors are used to divide a large room into smaller areas. The door panels in 4-27 are four feet (1220mm) wide and run on a track mounted on the ceiling and a guide in the floor (4-26). These are manually opened. However, some large installations are moved by an electric motor drive.

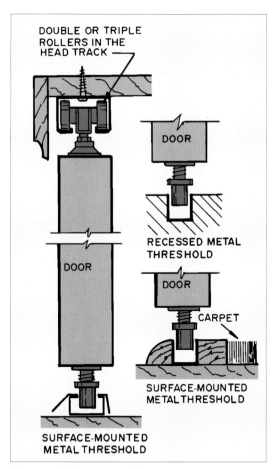

4-26 Bifold and multifold doors run better if a floor guide is used. However, the guide is not necessary for them to function. Thes guides are typically recessed made of metal, or surfae-mounted metal or wood.

4-27 Multifold doors are often used to divide a large room into several smaller areas. This door has large panels and folds into a pocket in the wall.

TABLE 4-7 COMMON HIGH-DOOR SIZES

Thickness	1¾"
Height	8'-2"
Width	
Single door	2'-0", 2'-6", 2'-8", 3'-6"
Double doors	4'-0", 5'-0", 5'-4", 6'-0"

HIGH DOORS

High doors are used on both exterior and interior door openings when the ceiling is nine feet or more and a more dramatic, higher opening is wanted. High doors are eight feet high (**4-28**). Commonly available sizes are given in **Table 4-7**. They are often used as double doors on a wide opening, and sidelights are available (**4-29**).

POCKET DOORS

Pocket doors are used when the swing of a hinged door is blocked, preventing it from fully opening, or when it would be an obstacle to the area when it is in an open position. The door slides into a frame built in the wall cavity (**4-30**). One type of framing built on the job is shown in **4-31**. Hardware manufacturers have a complete installation kit containing the studs, track, and related hardware (**4-32**).

4-28 This fiberglass eight-foot-high entry door with sidelights make a dramatic front entrance.

Courtesy Therma-Tru Doors

4-29 Such high doors are often used in pairs to increase the emphasis of the front entry and provide a focal point for the house.

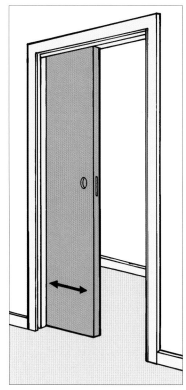

4-30 Pocket doors slide into the wall cavity.

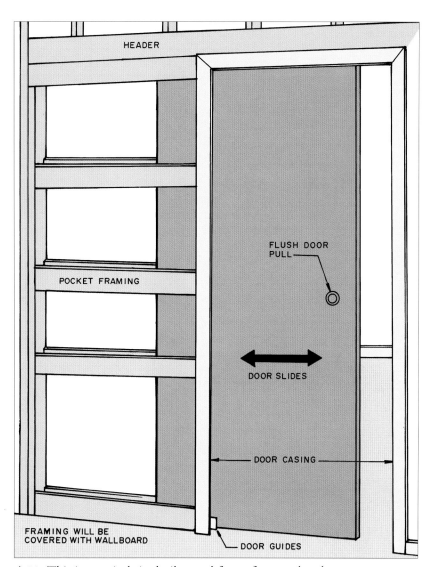

HEADER

FLUSH DOOR PULL

POCKET FRAMING

DOOR SLIDES

DOOR CASING

FRAMING WILL BE COVERED WITH WALLBOARD

DOOR GUIDES

4-31 This is a typical site-built wood frame for a pocket door.

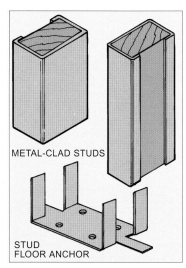

METAL-CLAD STUDS

STUD FLOOR ANCHOR

4-32 (Above and Right) Typical hardware available with a manufacturer-supplied pocket door installation. The actual design will vary with the manufacturer.

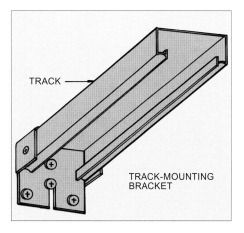

TRACK

TRACK-MOUNTING BRACKET

DOOR HANGER

TYPES OF RESIDENTIAL DOOR

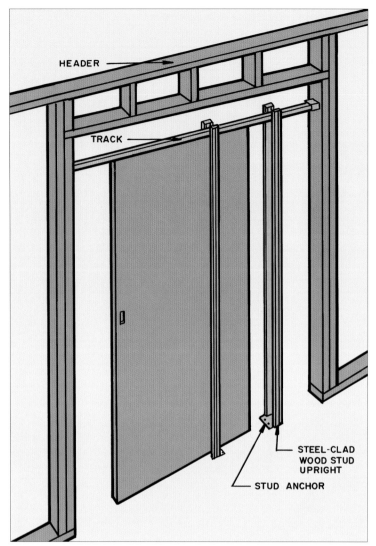

4-33 The pocket-door studs are connected to the overhead framing and secured to the floor.

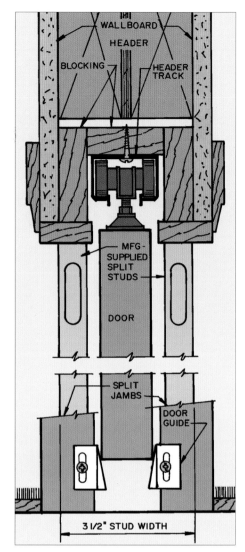

4-34 Typical installation detail for a pocket door. Notice the adjustable guides at the floor.

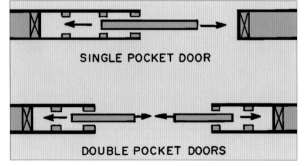

4-35 Single or double converging pocket-door installations are available.

The studs for pocket doors are installed as shown in 4-33. The door runs on an overhead track. Rollers are mounted on the top of the door. The bottom is controlled by guides (4-34).

Pocket doors can be single or double. Double doors slide into the opposite walls (4-35). They use standard doors as on other openings. When you secure hardware, be certain the doors you select will function with it.

DUTCH DOORS

Dutch doors have been used for many years and originally were used in barns (4-36). Dutch doors look like a standard hinged door. The difference is that they are separated into two small doors at the meeting rail (4-37). The top half can be left open while the bottom half prevents animals from leaving the building. When used in residences, a shelf is often built on the top edge of the lower door (4-38). The joining rails on exterior doors are weatherstripped. Each door may have a lockset. However, some put a dead bolt on the top door and a lockset on the lower door. Either way, both doors can be locked.

4-36 Dutch doors are associated with barns built many years ago.

4-37 Dutch doors are two small separate doors joining at the center lock rail. They are used as interior and exterior doors.

4-38 Dutch doors often have a shelf located at the top of the lower door. On exterior doors it is lowered a little below the door edge so the weatherstripping clears it. On interior doors the shelf is placed in a rabbet on top of the edge grain.

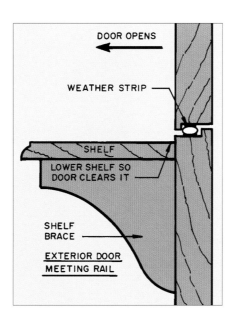

DOOR OPENS

WEATHER STRIP

SHELF

LOWER SHELF SO DOOR CLEARS IT

SHELF BRACE

EXTERIOR DOOR MEETING RAIL

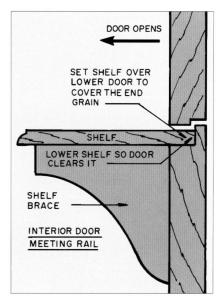

DOOR OPENS

SET SHELF OVER LOWER DOOR TO COVER THE END GRAIN

SHELF

LOWER SHELF SO DOOR CLEARS IT

SHELF BRACE

INTERIOR DOOR MEETING RAIL

STORM DOORS

Storm doors are installed on the outside of the exterior doorframe so they protect the entry door from the weather (**4-39**). This reduces deterioration and protects the finish. It also increases the energy efficiency of the door and provides security against unwanted entry. On pleasant days the standard door can be left open and the storm door will admit natural light into the house (**4-40**).

The airspace between the storm door and the entry door may trap excess heat and moisture under certain conditions. This could lead to damage to the finish of the entry door, so some storm doors are made with a small vent to allow the passage of these if they build up.

Storm doors are available in solid wood, vinyl, aluminum, and particleboard clad with aluminum. Some typical designs available are shown in **4-41**.

The glass in some storm doors can be removed and replaced with a screen (**4-42**). Some doors provide a space so that when the panel is not being used it slides down into the lower section of the door. Possibly the most popular type is one that is totally glazed, providing a full view of the exterior (**4-43**) with an expensive front entry door that adds to the appearance of the entryway.

4-39 Storm doors protect the expensive front door and provide additional energy efficiency.

4-40 A storm door also permits natural light to enter the foyer on pleasant days.

4-41 (Right) A few designs of storm doors commonly available.

REMOVE THE GLASS PANEL

INSTALL THE SCREEN PANEL

4-42 This aluminum storm door permits the glass panel to be removed and a screen panel to be inserted, providing ventilation.

4-43 This full-view storm door protects the entry door, yet provides natural light to the foyer and a view of the outside.

TYPES OF RESIDENTIAL DOOR

GARAGE DOORS

The principal type of **garage door** that is used in residential construction runs on tracks that carry the door up and across the ceiling (4-44). It is referred to as an overhead door. Made in sections about 20 inches (508mm) wide hinged on the edges, the door is moved by a chain drive or a spiral drive rod powered by an electric motor (4-45). The doors are operated by a remote control (4-46) kept in the automobile and a wall-mounted switch (4-47). Garage doors have a code that can be programmed in to foil thieves. Some have a keypad mounted outside the house. Entrance is obtained by pushing the numbered keypad buttons in the secret code sequence (4-48). The code can be changed whenever necessary.

Garage doors are heavy and, when lowered under power, they can damage a car or injure a person who may be in the way. The opener should have a sensor system that automatically reverses the closing motion of the door if it detects something in the way of the door's downward path. This is typically a photo-cell obstruction detector. If the path of the ray is broken, the door stops and reverses the downward motion.

On the end of the door-opener power unit are various controls used to adjust the opener systems, such as load the security code for the remote control and adjust the opening and closing movement (4-49).

Some have the sections designed so that a person cannot get his or her finger trapped between the closing panels (4-50). Another feature is a light. It comes on automatically as the door is opened and stays on for a few minutes, permitting those entering to open the door to the house under lighted conditions (4-51). The door should have a weather-tight seal along the bottom edge to block out moisture, air, and tiny creatures (4-52). A seal along the sides is also recommended to keep out air and moisture.

4-44 Overhead garage doors run on wheels in a curved track that carries the doors up along the ceiling.

4-45 Overhead doors are moved by a chain or spiral drive rod powered by an electric motor.

4-46 The garage door can be opened from the outside by signals sent by a remote control carried in the automobile.

4-47 The garage door can be opened with a wall-mounted switch that is usually located near the door that leads from the house into the garage.

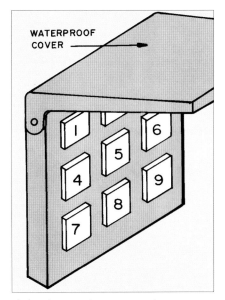

4-48 An exterior-mounted keypad can be used to open the garage door when the correct code is punched in on the numbered buttons.

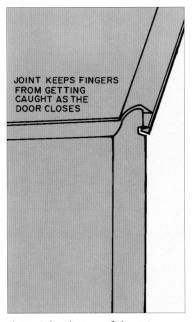

4-50 The design of the joint between the door sections should push the fingers out of the way as the door closes to prevent their getting caught between the doors.

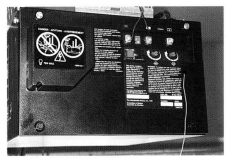

4-49 On the end of the door-opener power unit are adjustments used to regulate the operation of the door.

4-51 The garage-door opener has a light that remains on for several minutes after the door is opened.

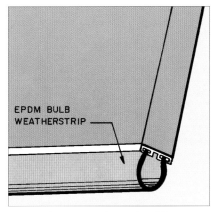

4-52 The garage door should have a weather-tight seal at the bottom of the door.

The door has an emergency release cord that allows the opener to be disengaged from the power drive and manually opened or closed. This is essential when the power is off or the door-opener mechanism is not functioning (4-53).

Overhead garage doors are available in wood, steel, insulated steel, fiberglass, and fiber-composite materials. The steel door is less expensive. In cold climates it should be insulated. Insulation is valuable in the summer and winter if a more moderate air temperature is wanted in the garage. Also consider insulating the walls and ceiling the same as those of the house. Garage doors are available in a variety of raised panel arrangements and as flush doors (4-54). Many have a wood-grain- or stucco-texture finished

4-53 This cord is pulled to release the door from the drive mechanism so it can be manually opened or closed when the door opener will not operate.

surface. Steel doors should have a galvanized coating over the steel and the baked-on enamel coating over this.

Steel doors are available for one-car and two-car openings as well as for a smaller opening for things such as golf carts, lawn mowers, and small tractors (4-55, 4-56, and 4-57). Typical sizes for garage doors are given in **Table 4-8**. Some companies will custom-make the size that you specicfy. Two-car garage doors should be at least 16'-0", but 18'-0" is a better width for ease of use. Single-car garage doors should be at least 8'-0", but 9'-0" is better (4-58). If a sport utility vehicle or large pickup truck is to be in the garage, check the manufacturer's dimensions of the vehicle before choosing a door width or height.

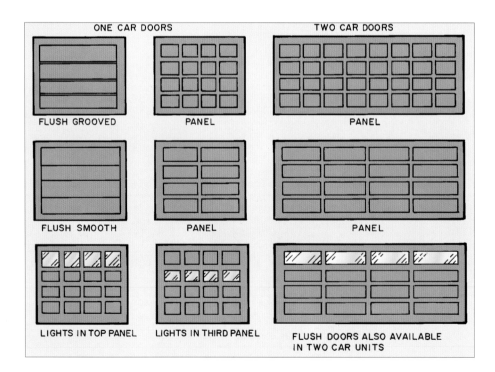

4-54 Garage doors are available in a number of raised-panel arrangements and as flush doors.

TABLE 4-8 TYPICAL GARAGE DOOR SIZES

Door height	6'-6", 6'-9", 7'-0", 8'-0"
Door width	4'-0", 6'-0", 8'-0", 9'-0", 10'-0", 12'-0", 16'-0", 18'-0", 20'-0"

4-55 This single door will admit two automobiles. One advantage is that it does not have the post between openings as is used with two single opening doors.

4-56 This garage has two one-car doors. One problem is having to avoid striking the post between them.

4-57 This garage has a single double door and a separate smaller door that might be used for golf carts and lawn mowers.

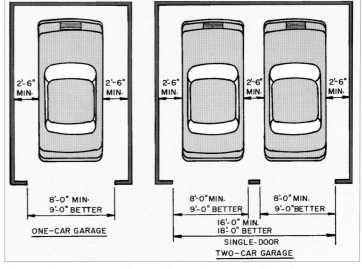

4-58 Whenever possible, use the widest garage door that you can accommodate. Typical-sized doors will handle typical two-door and four-door sedans.

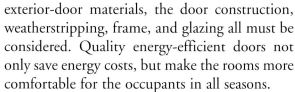

Glazing & Energy Efficiency

When plans are being drawn up for the design or remodeling of a house, any decisions that are made related to exterior doors will impact the energy efficiency of the building. In addition to the placement of the door, the exterior-door materials, the door construction, weatherstripping, frame, and glazing all must be considered. Quality energy-efficient doors not only save energy costs, but make the rooms more comfortable for the occupants in all seasons.

In the winters the exterior doors must reduce the heat loss to the exterior and, in the summer, reduce heat gain to the interior. This becomes even more important when the doors have considerable glazing, such as for patio or French doors (**5-1** and **5-2**).

TYPES OF GLASS

Door manufacturers offer a number of choices of glazing materials. Their standard doors will have certain types specified. Some will custom-build doors and can then install glazing materials, such as spectrally selective or reflective glass, that are not normally available. The advantages and disadvantages fo the common types of glass should be considered as decisions are made. Following is information about the process of glass-making and the various common types of glass available, including float (annealed) glass, tempered glass, heat-treated glass, tinted glass, spectrally selective glass, and reflective glass.

Courtesy Therma-Tru Doors

5-1 These patio doors have a large glazed area that has energy-efficient glazing to reduce heat transfer through the glass.

FLOAT (ANNEALED) GLASS

There are several types of glass manufactured. The type that is typically used in doors is a **soda-lime-silica** type. It is the least desirable because, when it is struck, it will shatter into sharp fragments, and it does not perform well under low temperatures or rapid temperature changes. It is not used in large pieces on doors and, in some cases, its use may be prohibited.

The type of glass used for windows and doors is **float glass**. It is made by floating the molten glass across a bath of molten tin. This produces a smooth, flat surface. It moves into an annealing lehr (oven) where the temperature is carefully lowered; it cools and rolls out in a long sheet, which is cut into the desired sizes. This process is called **annealing,** and float glass is often referred to as **annealed glass.**

Courtesy Weather Shield Manufacturing Company

5-2 French or patio doors should have adequate energy efficiency to minimize heat transfer through the large glass area.

TEMPERED & HEAT-TREATED GLASS

Tempered glass is used when standard annealed glass is not strong enough. Tempering involves raising the temperature of the glass almost to the softening point and then chilling it by blowing jets of cold air on both sides. Tempered glass is three to five times as resistant to damage as standard annealed glass. If it is broken, it falls in rounded, rather smooth pieces, reducing the danger of serious cuts.

Heat-treated glass is strengthened by heating and is then cooled as described for tempered glass. It has about the same strength as that of standard annealed glass.

TINTED GLASS

Glass is tinted by color-producing ingredients that are added to the molten glass in the glass-making furnace. The color is not a surface coating, but is consistent throughout the thickness of the glass. The color may vary some with the thickness of the glass. The degree of tint affects the solar-heat gain, light transmittance, and other properties. For each color and thickness of glass, the manufacturer provides specifications of such data.

The tint absorbs some the natural light and solar heat. In doing so, it reduces glare within the room from brilliant sunlight and reduces the transmission of solar heat.

Tinted glass has adequate transparency from the inside looking out. During the day it provides some privacy when viewed from the outside of the house. At night it is difficult to see outside from the inside and easier to see inside from the outside.

Tinted glass is made to absorb selected parts of or all of the solar spectrum and, therefore, to absorb heat. This heat develops within the glass, raising its temperature. A lot of this heat is radiated and then convected into the room, so that the amount of solar-heat reduction is not as great as with other types of glazing. It is much better at reducing glare than reducing heat.

SPECTRALLY SELECTIVE GLASS

Spectrally selective glass is a coated glass with optical properties that are transparent to selected wavelengths of energy and reflective to others.

Such glass is transparent to visible light and reflective to shortwave and longwave infrared radiation. Spectrally selective coatings filter out 40 to 70 percent of the heat that normally would be transmitted through clear glass, yet allow the full amount of natural light into the house.

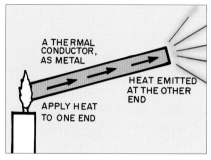

5-3 Heat applied to a material moves through it by conduction.

REFLECTIVE GLASS

Reflective glass has one surface covered with thin transparent layers of metallic film. The film is placed on the inside surface of the glass on single-glazed lights and, on double-glazed lights, on the side of the inside glass that faces the exterior—thus, it is inside the airspace cavity.

Reflective glass reduces the amount of solar energy transmitted through the glass. Typically 85 to 90 percent of solar energy is reflected to the outside. Reflective coatings reduce invisible as well as visible light transmittance into the house. From the outside, doors with reflective glass appear to be mirrors because they reflect the light from outside in the same manner as a mirror.

HEAT TRANSFER

Heat is transferred by conduction, radiation, convection, and air infiltration.

Thermal conduction is a process of heat transfer through a material in which kinetic energy is transmitted particle to particle through the material without actual displacement of the particles (5-3). Heat will pass through the door stiles, rails, panels, glazing, and frame by conduction. The greater the temperature difference between the exterior and interior air the faster the heat will be conducted.

Glass is a good thermal conductor, so it is especially important to use energy-efficient glazing to reduce heat-loss. A single glass pane may have only a few degrees difference between its outside surface temperature and the inside surface temperature. In cold weather this glass will conduct considerable heat out of the house and, in the summer, conduct heat inside (5-4). This increases energy costs and occupant discomfort. You can control conduction through glazing by using energy-efficient glazing. Storm doors can reduce heat loss and gain some, but more-efficient exterior doors are the best solution.

5-4 Glass is a good conductor of heat. Heat is transferred through it by conduction.

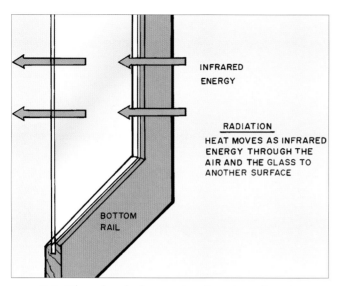

5-5 Glass absorbs heat and radiates it to the other side and on into the room.

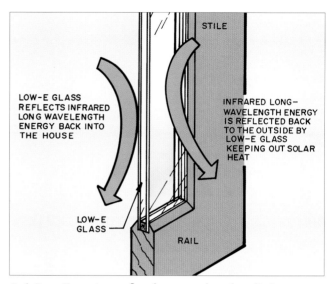

5-6 Low-E coatings reflect long-wavelength radiation, keeping out solar heat and retaining interior heat.

The doorframe exposes quite a few square inches to the exterior conditions. It can be a source of heat loss and gain. Wood and vinyl frames are more energy efficient than metal.

Radiation is the transfer of heat as infrared electromagnetic waves through the glass. It moves from a warmer source to a cooler surface (**5-5**). As radiation moves toward the cooler surface, it does not heat the air, but rather heats whatever it strikes, such as a chair or person. Glass absorbs heat and radiates it to the other side. If you sit near a door with a large glazed area, your body radiates heat to the colder glass, making you feel cold.

Part of the sun's energy is visible. The **shorter wavelengths** are beyond purple and are termed **ultraviolet** (UV), while the **longer wavelengths** which are beyond the red part of the visible spectrum of the

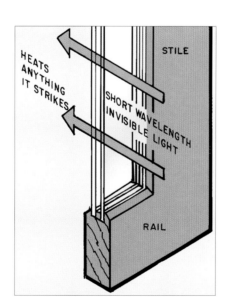

5-7 Short-wavelength visible light passes through the glass, heating anything it strikes.

sun's energy are termed **infrared** and are felt as heat. As the sun strikes the glass, heat, UV, and visible light enter the room. Here they may be absorbed and radiated into the room or reflected to other parts of the area.

Long-wavelength radiant-heat loss or gain can be overcome somewhat by placing a low-E coating on the glass. This coating reflects the infrared wavelengths (**5-6**). Short-wavelength visible light that passes through the glass to the interior will be absorbed by interior surfaces that it strikes, and the heat that is gained will be radiated as heat (**5-7**). This heat gain can be reduced, if desired, by lowering blinds or closing draperies over the windows, blocking the visible light. However, such heat gain may be desirable in the winter, providing a source of solar heat as well as natural light.

Convection occurs when air gives up heat to a cooler surface, such as the door glazing (5-8). The cooler air sinks to the floor, pulling new warmer air against the cold glass or door interior and creating a draft within the room. If a person is seated near a door with considerable glass, this draft will be very noticeable and uncomfortable. This draft can be reduced somewhat by placing insulated draperies or shades over the door and by using energy-efficient glazing and insulated doors.

Infiltration is the leakage of air through poorly fitting door assemblies. The doorframe should be caulked around the edges where it butts against the walls (5-9). A very small gap, over a number of hours, will permit a large volume of air to enter the house. Quality doors and frames that will not bow or warp and that have adequate weatherstripping are required.

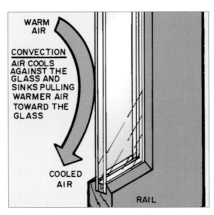

5-8 Convection occurs when air gives up heat to a cooler surface.

CONDENSATION

Condensation is the formation of moisture on a surface. On doors this will be most apparent on the glazing (5-10). Even energy-efficient glazing will, under certain conditions, be subject to having condensation form on it (5-11). This is due to the high humidity of the interior air, not necessarily a defect in the door glazing. The thing to do is reduce the level of humidity in the air in the house. About 30 to 50 percent relative humidity is recommended.

Under certain conditions the condensation can freeze on the interior of the door glazing.

Manufacturers of glazing often have it tested to find its **Condensation Resistance Factor** (**CRF**). Areas where it is seasonally very cold require glazing with a CRF rating of 35. Warmer climates can use units with a lower value.

PERFORMANCE DATA

Some manufacturers have their doors tested by independent laboratories that certify that the doors are manufactured to the American Architectural Manufacturers Association (AAMA) and Window and Door Manufacturers Association (WDMA) specifications. Additional tests include air-infiltration rates, water penetration, and structural pressure in pounds per square foot (psf). Air-infiltration tests show that wood-framed doors are more efficient at blocking air leakage than metal-framed doors, because metal expands and contracts more than wood. Many metal doors are built with a wood frame, as shown earlier in Chapter 3.

Air leakage around a door produces a much larger heat loss than the heat loss through the material of the door itself. Weatherstripping systems are critical to the energy efficiency of a door assembly.

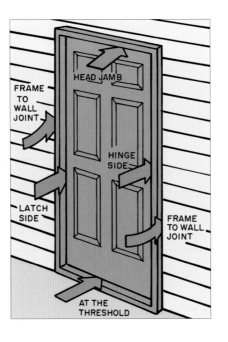

5-9 Air infiltration is a major source of heat loss and gain, and occurs around the edges of the door and the doorframe.

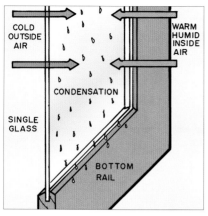

5-10 When the single glazing on door lights is cold, the humid inside air is likely to lead to condensation.

TABLE 5-1 THERMAL TRANSMISSION OF DOORS

Wood doors	U-factor
1¾" wood-panel door with 1⅛"-thick panels	0.40
1¾" solid-core wood flush door	0.34
Steel doors	
1¾" hollow-core steel door	0.58
1¾" insulated steel door (no thermal break)	0.42
1¾" insulated steel door (with thermal break)	0.20
Fiberglass doors (Values are similar to wood doors)	

Air infiltration is measured under controlled conditions, at a specified pressure difference between the air inside and outside the building. Leakage is expressed in cubic feet per minute per square foot of the total area. Lower rating numbers indicate a more airtight door. Many doors test at 0.10- to 0.20-cubic-feet-per-minute infiltration. Air infiltration will vary depending on the speed of the wind striking the door.

Water-resistance ratings indicate the capacity of the door to resist the penetration of water. The rating is measured as the maximum pounds per square foot (psf) at which no penetration will occur. Typical ratings vary from 3 to 15 psf.

Structural testing reveals the pressure that a door can resist in pounds per square foot. Typical ratings run from 30 to 90 psf.

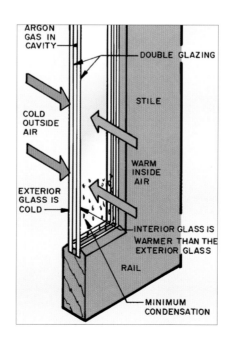

5-11 Energy-efficient glazing will, under conditions of high humidity, have some condensation form, but this is very unusual.

Performance standards for some types of door are available from the American Architectural Manufacturers Association (AAMA), the Window and Door Manufacturers Association (WDMA) and the American Society for Testing and Materials.

The energy efficiency of a door and its glazing is specified by its **U-factor**. The U-factor is a measure of the rate of heat flow through a material or an assembly of materials. It is the rate of nonsolar heat flow through the glazing and the door stiles, rails, and core. The U-factor is expressed in British Thermal Units (BTU) per hour per square foot of surface per degree of Fahrenheit (F) or watts per square meter per degree Celsius (C) per degree difference between the inside and outside surfaces. Some doors have a U-factor rating that includes the frame, glazing, and door. Some typical U-factor values are given in **Table 5-1**. These values show the thermal transmission through the door.

TABLE 5-2 TYPICAL U-FACTORS FOR SINGLE- & DOUBLE-GLAZED GLASS UNITS

	Center of glass U-factor	Unit U-factor	Percent relative humidity when moisture forms at the center of the glass
Single-glazed	1.10	0.80	14
Double-glazed	0.25	0.30	66

ENERGY-EFFICIENT GLAZING

Typical energy-efficient glazing for doors is usually a double-glazed light. A comparison of the U-factor of single- and double-glazed lights is given in **Table 5-2**. The difference in heat gained by these glass lights is given in **Table 5-3**.

INSULATING GLASS

Insulating glass is a glazing unit consisting of two or more layers of glass with an airspace between them. The edges are sealed so that the airspace is airtight. The edges of the glass are separated by an edge-spacer bonded to the glass. A sealant or glue is used around the perimeter to contain the glazing gas and ensure that the assembly is watertight. The spacer contains a desiccant material that absorbs any traces of moisture left in the airspace after the unit has been sealed. If the spacer is a metal gasket that touches the glass, heat and cold are convected through it reducing the efficiency at the edges of the glazing. To reduce this loss, manufacturers are using a variety of edge-spacers made from materials that have insulating value. One type uses a silicone foam spacer containing desiccant. It has adhesive on the edges to seal it to the glass **(5-12)**. Another uses a silicone rubber spacer. When metal spacers are used, they are separated from the glass with a sealant or the thermal break is placed in the center of the spacer.

TABLE 5-3 TYPICAL HEAT GAINS FOR CLEAR GLASS

Clear glazing	Heat gain $(Btu/ft^2/hr)$
Single pane ⅛"	214
Single pane ³⁄₁₆"	208
Double pane	186

The airspace is usually filled with argon or krypton gas. This provides a degree of insulation which reduces the transmission of heat and cold through the airspace.

In areas of high wind or unusually high temperatures that cause stress on the glass, insulating glass units are made that use heat-strengthened or tempered glass. They are available with tinted, reflective, laminated, and low-E glass.

GAS FILLS

The efficiency of multiple-glazed windows is improved by replacing the air in the cavities with a gas that has a lower conductivity than air. The gases used are inert. **Inert gases** are a group of chemically stable, nonreactive gases that occur naturally in the atmosphere. If the window were broken and the gases released into the atmosphere, the gases would be harmless.

The most commonly used gas is **argon**. It is effective and inexpensive. Another gas used is **krypton**. It is better for reducing heat loss than argon but is more expensive. Krypton is often used in triple- and quadruple-glazed units; because being more energy efficient, the width of the cavity can be reduced. Argon-filled glazing cavities are typically ½ inch. The gas does not affect visible light transmittance.

A well-made, properly sealed, multiple-glazed unit will retain the gas for many years. Some manufacturers use a dual seal around the edge of the unit. A dual seal is more likely to retain the gas in the unit longer that a single seal.

When argon or krypton gas fills the cavities of a multiglazed unit that has a low-E coating, the heat transmission by conduction and convection is greatly reduced. This reduces summer heat gain and winter loss. Since the interior glass is warmer, condensation is less likely to occur.

LOW-E COATINGS

The efficiency of the glazing can be improved by using glass with a **low-E coating**. Refer to **5-6**, on page 61. This coating is a microscopically thin metal or metal oxide layer applied to the surface of the glass. This type of coating is almost invisible. Typical low-E coatings are transparent to the visible spectrum and also allow the transmission of shortwave infrared radiation. The low-E coating, however, is effective at reflecting longwave infrared radiation and limiting the emission of radiant energy. This suppression of infrared radiation increases the energy efficiency of the glazing, thus giving a reduced value for the U-factor. This type of coating permits a high level of natural light transmission. These coatings are especially valuable on glass doors and doors with considerable glazing.

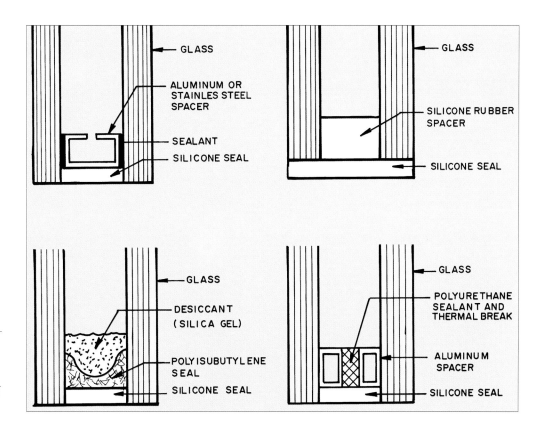

5-12 Double-glazed lights are made with several types of edge spacer.

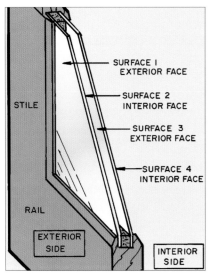

5-13 The glazing surfaces of the unit are identified by number.

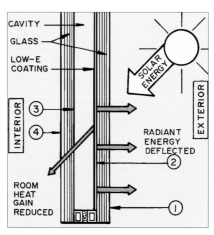

5-14 In areas where air-conditioning is important, the low-E coating is placed on the inside of the exterior glass (surface 2) in double-glazed insulating units.

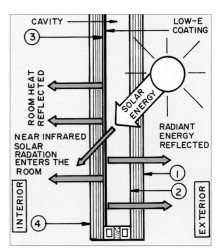

5-15 Where heating is the major consideration, the low-E coating is placed on the inside of the interior glass (surface 3).

Low-E coatings can be applied to either of the interior surfaces of the glass in double-glazed units. The surfaces are numbered as shown in **5-13**. Because some shortwave energy is absorbed by a low-E coating whether it is on surface 2 or 3, this affects its performance. Where cooling the air is most important, the coating is placed on surface 2 (**5-14**). This lowers the solar-heat-gain rating and reduces solar energy gains. Where heating is most important, the coating is located on surface 3 (**5-15**). This permits solar energy to pass through the exterior glazing and the cavity, putting the absorbed solar energy on the room side glass and increasing solar-heat gain in the room.

Low-E coatings may be **hard-coat** (pyrolitic) or **soft-coat** (sputtered). Generally soft coats have lower emissivities, so have higher insulation values, but do not admit as much solar heat as hard coats. Soft coats are easily damaged and are used only on the interior surfaces of double-glazed units. Hard coats are more durable and can be used on exposed surfaces. While they are thicker than soft coats, they are still very thin.

There are several types of low-E coating and they absorb and transmit different amounts of solar energy. If you live in a northern climate, choose one that admits sufficient solar energy to be useful in the winter yet blocks come heat gain in the summer.

Heat-transmission low-E coatings are used in northern areas. They permit the transmission of near infrared solar radiation and reflect the far infrared radiation (**5-15**). This provides for solar-heat gain in the winter and reduces heat loss from the inside to the exterior.

Selective-transmission low-E coatings are used on window glazing to be used in climates where both winter heating and summer cooling requirements are important. In the summer they admit natural light yet reduce solar infrared energy transmission. In the winter they reduce heat loss from the interior of the house. A typical example is shown in **5-14**.

Low-transmission low-E coatings are used in warm climates, allowing the smallest amount of solar-heat gain and reducing the amount of visible-light transmission to control glare.

Solar-control film is another product used to provide solar-heat control and ultraviolet-radiation control. The film is a polyester substrate with a special scratch-resistant coating on one side. It is applied to the interior surface of the glass, It reduces the transmittance of light and infrared heat through glass and has ultraviolet absorbers to reduce the amount of ultraviolet radiation transmitted through the glass, This product is placed on the door glazing after the doors are installed.

SAFETY & ACOUSTICAL GLAZING

As discussed earlier in this chapter, tempered and heat-treated glass are much stronger than the float (annealed) glass commonly available. Doors are subject to considerable hard use and occasionally someone will walk into a glass door not realizing it is closed and blocking their path. Building codes typically require specific types of glass in all exterior doors. Some additional products to consider are laminated glass, acoustical glass, and safety film.

LAMINATED GLASS

Laminated glass is used in areas where extra protection against breakage is needed. A hurricane-prone area is one place where this glass would help give protection against flying debris (**5-16**). Laminated glass consists of the bonding of layers of float glass with interlayers of plasticized polyvinyl butyral (PVB) resin or polycarbonate (PC) resin. The glass is chemically strengthened by immersion in a molten salt bath. Should it be broken, the

5-16 This entryway is glazed with laminated glass that is more break-resistant than tempered glass. This provides security against storms and break-ins. It also has desirable sound-transmission properties.

Courtesy ODL

polyvinyl butyral interlayer keeps the glass intact so that there is no interior damage. This glazing also reduces noise transfer and ultraviolet radiation into the room. It reduces the chance of an intruder breaking and entering the house though it. The frame used must be strong enough to resist the same damaging forces as the glass.

ACOUSTICAL GLASS

Acoustical glass is a form of laminated glass. It has a layer of sound-absorbing plastic bonded between layers of glass. The soft plastic interlayer permits the glass panels to bend slightly in response to the pressure from sound waves. It is also available in multiglazed insulated units.

Two panes separated by an airspace are better than a single pane. The thicker the glass, the better it resists sound transmission. Wider airspaces will have a greater sound-transmission loss. Some units use a glass pane and a plastic pane with an airspace. Of course, the door must be tightly sealed. Sound as well as air can filter in around a poorly fitting door. Generally a sound level for residences of 30 to 40 dBA (decibel scale) is recommended. The rating system used for describing the sound-transmission properties gives a single number that is identified as the **Sound Transmission Class (STC)**.

SAFETY FILM

Safety film is a thin plastic film that is applied to provide some protection when the glazing is shattered by holding the shards, preventing them from flying in the air. This is valuable in particular situations, such as during a storm in which objects can become projectiles blown against the glass, shattering it. The safety film does reduce visible light transmittance and may slightly obscure the view.

5-17 The glass in the entry is a combination of crystalline glue-chip and clear beveled glass. Round brass caming is in the bevel, highlighting the geometric shapes.

Courtesy Therma-Tru Doors

DECORATIVE GLASS

A number of manufacturers produce decorative glass lights. These are available as door lights and as sidelights. The fiberglass entry door in **5-17** has lights made from clear beveled glass and crystalline glue-chip glass. They are framed with a polished brass caming. **Caming** is a strip—such as lead, zinc, or brass—that is bonded to the glass, forming a decorative pattern. A door light with frosted glass is seen in **5-18**. A delicate pattern is formed on the glass by frosting the background and leaving the pattern on the clear glass. Another approach is shown in **5-19**. Here the glass has a six-color image developed on it using a texture silk-screen process. This enables the use of several colors to create an elegant entryway. Still another product bonds vibrant acrylic colors permanently to the glass (**5-20**). It appears much like a stained-glass window. The light in **5-21** uses a swirled baroque glass. The design cluster has curved bevels and rounded brass caming. The design is sealed between two panes of safety-tempered, insulating glass.

Many other designs and assembly techniques are available from door and glass manufacturers.

Courtesy Therma-Tru Doors

5-18 These doors have a double-paned safety-tempered glass that has a design outlined by a lightly frosted background.

Courtesy ODL

5-19 This door light has a six-color image developed on it using a texture silk-screen process. Each design has colors offset by clear glass.

Courtesy ODL

5-20 These lights are made by bonding acrylic colors to the glass to produce the appearance of stained glass.

5-21 This decorative glazing places a center cluster of curved bevels and brass caming between two panes of safety-tempered, insulating glass. This provides energy efficiency and security.

ACRYLIC BLOCKS

Acrylic blocks appear much like glass blocks but are considerably lighter and can be used to glaze door lights, sidelights, and transoms (**5-22** and **5-23**). They are available in scratch-resistant, high-quality acrylic units that will stand up against harsh weather and resist discoloration. Several surface patterns, such as a frosted finish and a clear, smooth surface, are available.

Acrylic blocks are made by hermetically sealing two cast pieces to create a cavity, providing an insulating airspace. The U-factor is about the same as for a typical double-glazed window.

5-22 Acrylic-block glazing units are used to glaze doors, sidelights, and transoms. They admit natural light yet provide privacy.

5-23 When standard doors are used, acrylic-block glazing can be used for sidelights and transoms. Considerable natural light is admitted into the foyer.

Hardware & Security

Choosing hardware is an important part of the process of selecting items that enhance the appearance of a home and the ease in which doors operate. The major entryway deserves an attractive, high-quality lockset that reflects the style of the house and is of a quality that will remain attractive and operate easily for years (**6-1**). Another consideration is security. The incidence of home break-ins is high enough that providing secure locking devices on exterior doors is important. Typically it takes an intruder only a couple of minutes to find a way to penetrate the average home. While many of these entries are through windows, secure doors deserve major consideration.

LOCKSETS

There are a variety of locksets available. Some are designed for use on interior doors where security is not as important. Exterior locksets that are key operated are stronger and provide the needed security. The level of security varies with the type of lock and the quality of its construction.

There are two commonly used kinds of lockset available, bored and mortised. **Bored locksets** come in two types that are easy to install. They require only two holes to be bored in the door. Also refer to installation details that are covered in Chapters 7 and 8. The two types of bored lockset are tubular and cylindrical.

Courtesy Baldwin Hardware Corporation

6-1 Quality entry locksets add to the overall impression of the front entrance and remain attractive and operate easily for many years.

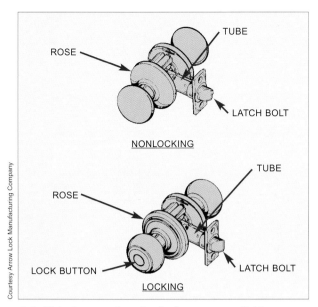

6-2 Tubular-type interior locksets are available as locking and nonlocking types.

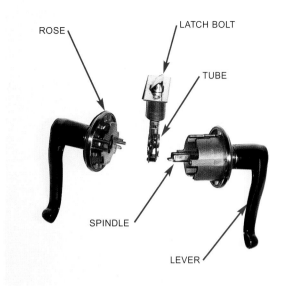

6-3 The latch bolt in the tube is operated by the spindle that is turned by the knob or lever handle.

TUBULAR & CYLINDRICAL BORED LOCKSETS

The **tubular-type lockset** (**6-2**) has a spring-loaded latch bolt inside a tube. The knobs or lever handles mount on a spindle that passes through an opening in the latch-bolt tube (**6-3**). When the knob or lever is turned, the latch bolt moves back into the tube, permitting the door to be opened.

Locksets used on interior doors are tubular type. Tubular-type exterior locksets are also available. Those on interior doors, such as for bedrooms and bathrooms, will have a means for locking for privacy, but can be opened from the outside in an emergency. They will have a locking button on the inside knob or lever that is pushed in to lock the door. It is unlocked from the inside merely by turning the handle. The outside knob or lever has a small hole into which a wire or nail can be inserted to unlock the door from outside the room. Other interior locksets will latch the door but cannot be locked. These are often referred to as **passage locks**. They are used for closets, storerooms, and other places where privacy is not required. Another type consists of just a knob or lever that is screwed to a door to serve as a pull (**6-4**). It is sometimes called a **dummy lock**. It is used on doors, such as bifolds, where a latch is not required. It is simply screwed to the face of the door. Generally the same style knob or lever is used on the other doors selected.

6-4 Dummy-lock knobs and levers are used on doors that do not need a latch bolt. They serve as a door pull. This one is on a bifold door.

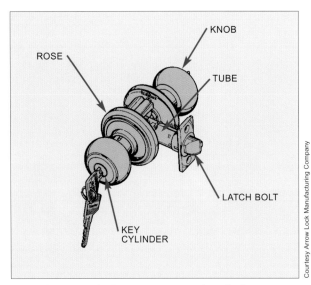

Courtesy Arrow Lock Manufacturing Company

6-5 This is a tubular-type exterior door lockset. It has a key cylinder in the outside knob and a lever to control the lock on the inside knob.

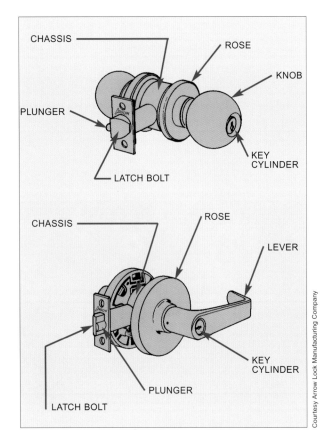

Courtesy Arrow Lock Manufacturing Company

6-6 Cylindrical locksets provide excellent security for exterior doors.

Tubular-type locksets are also available for use on exterior doors. They have a key control on the outside knob and a lever on the inside to lock and unlock the door (6-5). They are not as secure as cylindrical locks, which are recommended for use on exterior doors.

A **cylindrical lockset** is shown in **6-6**. It is installed in the same general manner as the tubular-type; however, it provides greater security. This type of lockset has a large-diameter cylinder called the chassis (**6-7**). The latch is secured into the side of the cylinder. The key cylinder is installed in the knob. A lever or pushbutton on the inside knob is used to lock and unlock the door from the inside.

The cylindrical and tubular locksets are available with a wide variety of knobs and lever handles. The lever handles are available in a straight shape and a variety of curved designs (**6-8**) and in a number of different finishes. The large variety of knob locksets also come in a number of different finishes (**6-9**). The lever-type handle has the advantage that it makes it easier to open the door. This is especially helpful for children and those who have some disability that makes turning a round knob difficult.

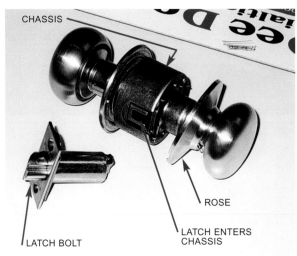

6-7 A typical cylindrical lockset.

6-8 Quite a variety of levers are available. Choose one that fits the interior décor of the house.

6-9 (Top, middle, and bottom right) These are a few examples of the many knobs available. When visiting the building supply dealer, be certain to view the total array of knobs.

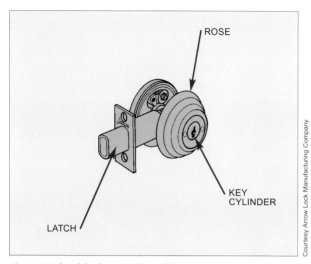

6-10 A dead bolt provides additional security.

Another widely used lock is the **dead bolt** (**6-10**). It is much like the lockset just described. However, it has a single metal latch that can be moved only by a key from the outside (**6-11**) or by an inserted key or thumb turn on the inside of the door (**6-12**). Some entry locksets have a dead bolt included in addition to the latch used to hold the door closed (**6-13**). A dead bolt is used to increase the security of the door. Some locksets with plungers can have the plunger pushed back with a plastic card, allowing the door to be opened. The dead bolt alongside the latch bolt prevents this from happening.

Single- and double-cylinder dead bolts are both available. A **single-cylinder dead bolt** has a key that operates it from outside and a thumb turn to operate it from the inside. This is quite adequate for residential use and, in some areas, it is the only type permitted by the local building code.

6-11 The dead bolt is operated by a key on the outside of the door.

6-12 This dead bolt has a thumb turn on the inside of the door.

Double-cylinder dead bolts require a key to open or close the lock from either side of the door. This prevents an intruder who has entered some other way from opening the door (**6-14**). Generally these locks are prohibited by local codes because, in an emergency, finding the key can be a problem and would keep the occupants from fleeing the building. Some want to use these to keep a potential intruder from opening the door by breaking the side glass or door light and reaching in to unlock the door, as could happen with a single-cylinder lock. It is better to provide security glazing over any glass than to use a double-cylinder lock.

Select a dead bolt that has a hardened steel bolt so that it cannot be cut through. The dead bolt should penetrate the doorjamb at least one inch and have and extra-strong strike plate that is secured with extra-long screws. It must be firm enough so that it cannot be torn away from the doorframe.

MORTISE LOCKSET

A **mortise lock** is a high-quality entryway lockset (**6-15**). It differs a great deal from bored locksets. It has an anti-friction latch and a hardened-steel saw-proof dead bolt. A mortise lock requires that a deep-pocket mortise be cut into the edge of the door to receive the mechanism.

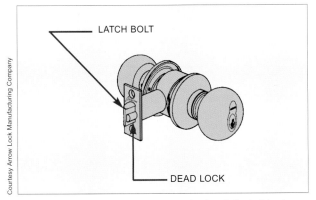

Courtesy Arrow Lock Manufacturing Company

6-13 A dead-bolt lock next to the latch bolt blocks attempts to slide the latch back with a plastic card.

6-14 This double-cylinder dead bolt requires that a key be used to unlock the door from the inside. It is usually mounted in tandem with a lever or knob lockset.

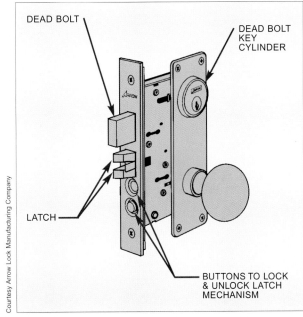

Courtesy Arrow Lock Manufacturing Company

6-15 A mortise lock has a latch bolt and a dead bolt.

Then several holes are bored through the face of the door for the key cylinder, knob spindle, and other controls (6-16 and 6-1). Follow the manufacturer's instructions, since designs vary. A view of the interior mechanism is shown in 6-17. This shows that the internal parts are fitted with clock like precision, giving long service, security, and trouble-free operation. Mortise locks are the very best units available.

The mortise lock also adds considerably to the overall appearance of the entryway. A variety of designs and finishes are available. One example is shown in 6-18.

Other entryway locksets have separate dead bolts and a latching handle-set assembly (6-19).

The dead bolt has a decorative rose behind the key cylinder. The handle-set assembly has a decorative escutcheon. Brass is a popular finish, though other finishes are available. Each is installed separately, much like the dead-bolt and bored-lockset installations shown in Chapter 7. The manufacturer supplies detailed installation instructions.

The locking mechanism for sliding glass doors is built into the unit at the factory. It has a hooked lever that fits into a metal packet, latching the door. An interior lever controls the operation (6-20). This is not very secure, and other security devices are needed to provide adequate protection.

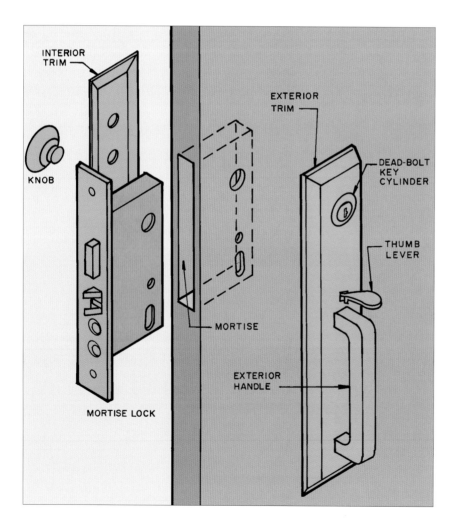

6-16 Mortise locks are set into a deep mortise pocket cut into the edge of the door.

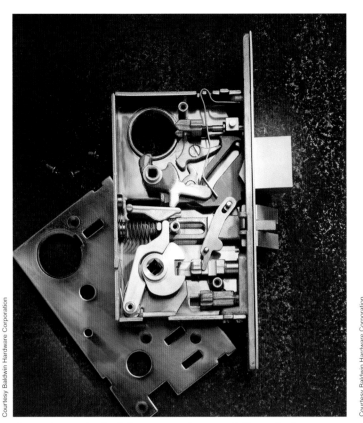

6-17 A mortise lock has a complex, carefully crafted internal mechanism that enables it to function smoothly for a very long time.

6-18 The exposed mortise trim plate sets the style of the entryway door and deserves major consideration as choices are considered.

6-19 A commonly used entryway lockset installation includes separate dead bolts and a latching handle set assembly.

6-20 Sliding-glass-door locks provide minimum security.

DOOR ACCESSORIES

A **door knocker** is an attractive addition to the entryway door (**6-21**). Various designs are available in brass and bronze and can be chosen to complement the style of the house. Since electric doorbells are almost always installed, these carryovers from an earlier time are mostly decorative.

Another accessory is a **kick plate** on the bottom edge of the door. This provides protection of the door, but, on residences, it is again mainly decorative (**6-22**).

6-21 Adoor knocker adds a decorative touch to the entryway door. It should complement the door-lockset escutcheon design.

Door closers are part of the hardware that is received with a storm door (**6-23**). They give protection from high winds by limiting the amount of outward swing, pulling the door closed, and cushioning the closing of the door. The hold-open washer permits the door to stand open when ventilation is wanted or an item needs to be moved through the entry and there is no hand free to hold the door.

Doorstops are used to keep the door from striking a wall or cabinet if opened too far. There are several types available (**6-24**).

6-22 Brass kick plates protect the door but mainly serve as a decorative feature.

6-23 Door closers should be mounted on the top and bottom rails of storm doors.

6-24 Doorstops are used to keep a door from swinging back and striking the wall. The type that mounts on a hinge is especially nice because it is up out of the way.

Courtesy Baldwin Hardware Corporation

The hinge-mounted stop is one of the most convenient doorstops because it does not stick out into the room.

HINGES

While hinges on most types of door are not seen, their selection is important. Cheap hinges are a poor investment. They get frequent use and carry a heavy door. Many doors used today come pre-hung on a doorframe. Be certain the hinge supplied is a quality product.

6-25 Butt hinges with rounded corners are used on interior doors.

The most commonly used hinge for exterior and interior doors is the **butt hinge**. The hinge with rounded corners is generally used on interior doors (**6-25**). The one with the square corner leaves is used on some exterior and interior doors (**6-26**). The hinge with one square corner and one round corner hinge is used on steel and fiberglass exterior doors (**6-27**).

Courtesy Baldwin Hardware Corporation

HINGE ON METAL DOOR

HINGE ON FIBERGLASS DOOR

6-26 Stylish square-corner butt hinges are often used on the exterior doors.

6-27 Steel and fiberglass doors are often hung with a hinge that has a round corner leaf mounted on the jamb and a square corner leaf on the door.

6-28 The pin on hinges used on interior doors can be removed, enabling the door to be removed.

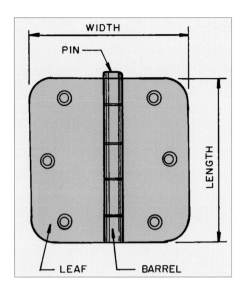

6-30 The size of a hinge is indicated by specifying the length of the leaf and the width in a flat open position.

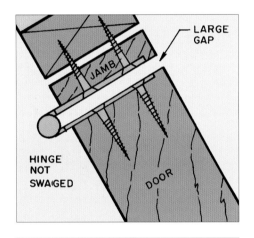

6-29 Door hinges are swaged, meaning the leaves are bent in such a way as to reduce the size of the space between the door and the jamb.

6-31 This hinge is used on bifold doors. It does not require a mortise and leaves a narrow crack.

6-32 This nonmortise hinge can be used to hang doors to the jamb. It leaves a very small crack between the door and jamb.

Hinges mounted on an interior door have a loose pin that enables you to remove the door by pulling the pin (**6-28**). Hinges on exterior doors should have the pin secured in place with another small pin inserted through the barrel into the pin. This prevents an intruder from removing the pin on exterior doors to gain access to the house. Heavy doors should use commercial-grade hinges or ball-bearing hinges. Heavy doors could have an extra hinge installed. Typical exterior and interior residential doors will have three hinges.

Hinges that are used on exterior and interior doors are swaged as shown in **6-29**. This reduces the size of the gap between the door and frame.

Hinges are specified by giving the length of the leaf parallel with the barrel and the width, which is measured when the hinge is open in a flat position (**6-30**). The width of the hinge chosen depends upon the thickness of the door. The various sizes available and some recommendations for selecting hinges are given in Chapter 7.

A typical hinge that is used on bifold doors in shown in **6-31**. It is a small nonmortise hinge. Since one leaf fits into the opening in the other leaf, only a very small gap exists between the doors.

Doors can be hung without mortises using a nonmortise hinge (**6-32**). The leaves are screwed to the edge of the door and jamb, leaving a very narrow gap the width of the thickness of the hinge leaf. If the doors are heavy, check to see whether they will carry the weight.

SECURITY

As mentioned earlier, quality locks, dead bolts, and strong hinges with nonremovable pins are an essential element in creating good deterrents for unwelcome intruders. There are a number of other measures that can be taken to increase security specifically in relation to doors. A **peephole** set through the door is a simple way to allow you to have a view of who is at the door before you unlock and open it (**6-33**).

Even better is installing a **video sentry system**, particularly one with a pushbutton tilt-control **camera** that provides color images of those at the door as well as the ability to talk with the person at the same time before opening your door (**6-34**).

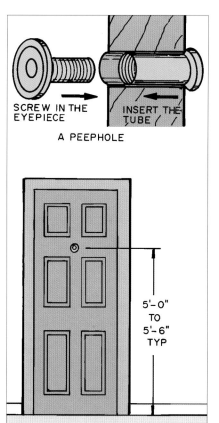

6-33 A peephole installed through an entry door lets you see who is there outside before you open it.

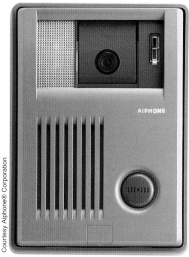

Courtesy Aiphone® Corporation

6-34 This is a color-video door station that is mounted on the door at the outside. The indoor unit has a tilt control that moves the lens from horizontal up forty degrees, twenty degrees up and down. The unit also has an audio system that permits you to communicate from inside the house with the person or persons outside the house while the door remains closed, before you decide to unlock it.

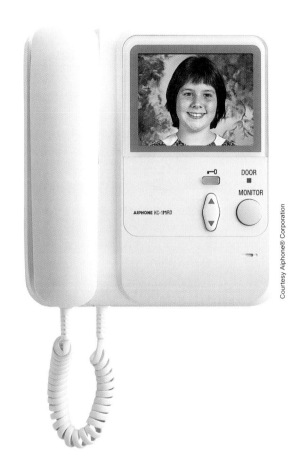

One camera can supply the same image to several **monitors** located in different rooms within the house (**6-35**). It also has a communication system allowing you to talk with the person at the door before you open it. The system will not only provide a color or black/white picture of the person at the door, but with the addition of a **picture memory unit** it will store images for replay. The image can include a time and date stamp of the viewing (**6-36**).

Another easy-to-install security device is a double-plate strike that replaces the single-thickness door strike. The double-strike back plate has a metal box into which the plunger from the door lockset fits (**6-37**).

6-35 (Left) This is the video master station mounted inside the house by the door. The long vertical button controls the angle of the lens on the exterior unit. The handset on the left side is used to communicate with the person outside the door.

6-36 The images stored by the picture memory unit have the date and time recorded.

You can also replace the screws in the hinge on the doorframe with longer screws (6-38). Use 3- or 3½-inch screws that will penetrate firmly into the stud behind the doorframe. If the door has sidelights, be careful that the length of the screws is not so great that they continue to into the stile and break the glass.

Garage doors are notoriously rather easy to force open and an intruder, once inside, is concealed from view. This makes it necessary that the door from the garage into the house be as secure as all the other exterior doors.

Allowing your pets access to the outdoors can be a security concern. See Chapter 8 for a discussion of secutiry and pet access doors.

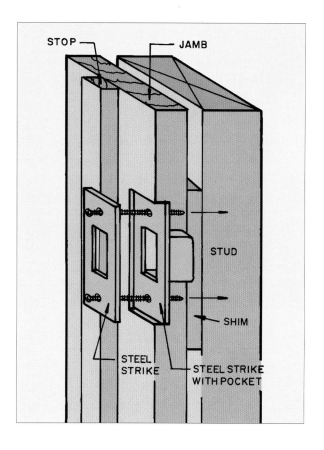

6-37 (Right) Making sure that you install a steel strike that has a pocket as well as a flat strike plate will provide additional protection against the possibility of an intruder's being able to force open or even break in the door.

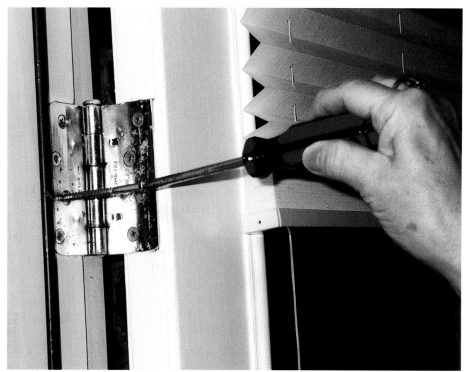

6-38 Replacing one or more of the ordinary-length hinge screws with screws that are long enough to enter firmly into the stud increases the security of the door.

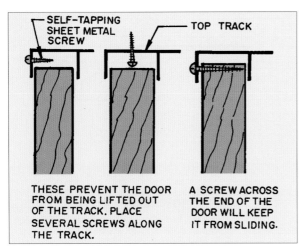

6-39 Sliding glass doors can be made more secure by installing sheet-metal screws to prevent them from being lifted off the track.

Sliding glass doors can be a major security problem. To increase their security, some types have been designed so that the sliding door cannot be simply lifted off the track to give entrance to the house. If the sliding door is an older type, screws can be installed along the top of the doorframe, preventing the door from being lifted out (6-39). Pins can also be set through holes drilled in the frame at the floor, blocking the door from sliding open (6-40). A wood stick or metal bar can be placed in the track on the floor (6-41). Commercial products are available, such as a long adjustable rod that is placed between the end of the door and the doorframe. A small clamp that is screwed to the frame at the floor is also available (6-42). Another security tip is to place steel plates at the lockset to keep someone from slipping a plastic card in the gap and opening the plunger. If the door opens into the house, an angle iron can be screwed to the doorframe with nonremovable screws (6-43). If the door swings out, a steel plate can be bolted to the door, as shown in 6-44. Use bolts with round heads or peen the end after the nut has been tightened to keep it from being unscrewed.

There are a number of door security devices that are secured to the inside of the door and connected to the doorframe (6-45). While these do not provide the protection given by a good lock, they do offer a deterrent.

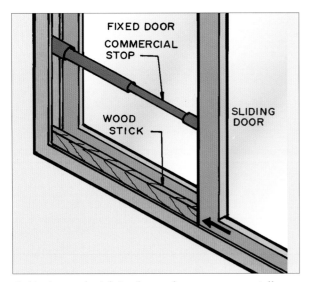

6-41 A wood stick in the track, or a commercially available stop rod, will prevent a sliding door from being forced open.

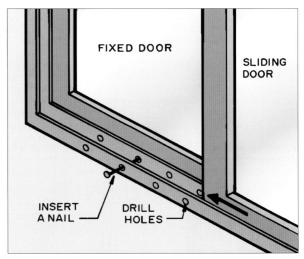

6-40 A series of holes drilled in the track will limit the amount the sliding door can be opened. The door can be open a little for ventilation but not forced open enough to permit entry.

6-42 This is a commercially available clamp that locks on the track, blocking the movement of a sliding door.

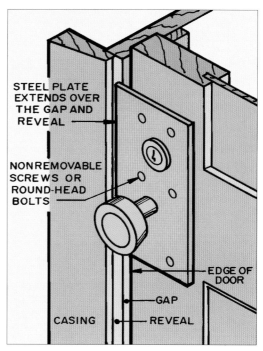

6-43 An angle iron installed beside the lock makes it difficult for a potential intuder to get to the latch and force it open. This is used on doors that open into a house or an apartment.

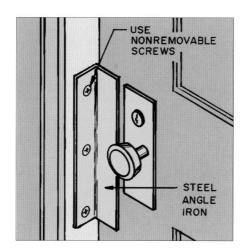

6-44 If the door opens out, bolt a metal escutcheon plate over the area surrounding the lock. Use screws that cannot be removed or run bolts that have raised heads through the door.

6-45 These are two of the several types of door-security devices that are available. These provide some security but are not a substitute for a quality door lock.

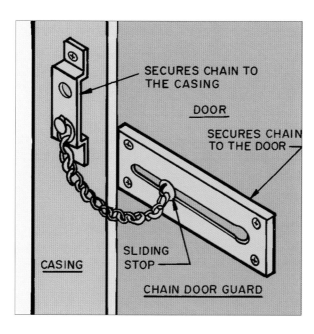

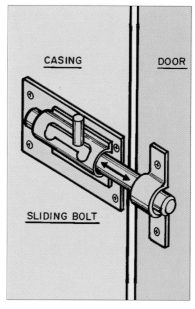

Another simple technique that can be used to keep a door with loose-pin hinges from being removed after the pins have actually been pulled but while the door is closed is shown in **6-46**.

ALARM SYSTEMS

Alarm systems are widely used to provide security for the house when occupied or unoccupied. Some send an alarm to the local police station or to a central monitoring site operated by the alarm company. They also can be set to just sound an alarm at the house and not notify authorities. The systems available included hard-wired and wireless installations.

HARD-WIRED ALARM SYSTEMS

A **hard-wired system** has a **control panel** (**6-47**) that has a transformer operating on 120 volts that converts the current to a low voltage. Switches used on doors and sensors used on windows are connected to the panel. The system operates on a closed circuit. When it is turned on, a low-voltage current flows through the wires connected to the door switches and window sensors. When a door or window is opened, the circuit is broken and the alarm is activated. The system has a **control pad** near the entrance doors generally used, such as the front door and the door from the garage (**6-48**). When you enter the house, the control typically has a 30-second delay before sounding the alarm, allowing you time to deactivate the system by punching in a code on the pad keys.

A mechanical switch that is sometimes used on swinging doors is much like that on a refrigerator door. Commonly they become unreliable due to corrosion. A better switch is a hermetically sealed unit with the switching device and magnet in one unit. The control ball on the end touches the edges of the door (**6-49**).

Another concealed type of switch has a magnet inserted in the edge of the door and a magnetic switch recessed into the door frame (**6-50**).

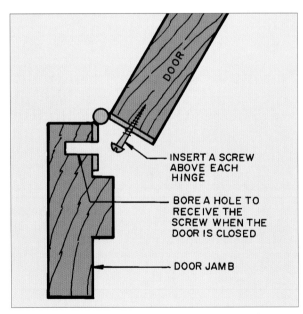

6-46 This is an easy way to prevent the door from being lifted out when the hinge pin has been removed.

6-47 This control panel operates a hard-wired security system. It is placed in a closet or other out-of-the-way location. A 120V transformer supplies 24V to the system.

6-48 This control pad is placed near the most frequently used exterior door and operates the system.

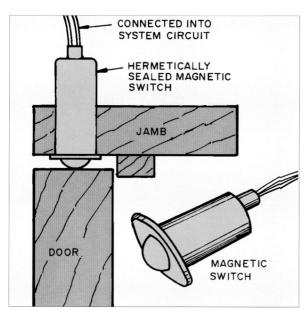

6-49 This ball-type switching device is placed into the doorframe and activates the alarm when the door is opened.

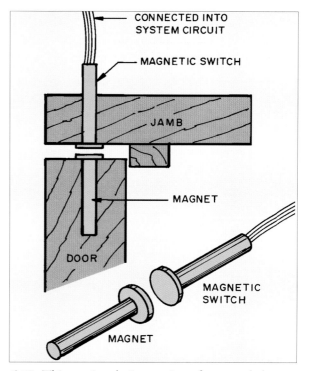

6-50 This sensing device consists of a concealed magnet switch in the jamb and a magnet inserted into the edge of the door.

A significant advantage of this type of switch is that the switch is not easily visible or noticeable, even when the door is open (**6-51**).

Surface-mounted sensors are sometimes used. The magnet is mounted on the door and the switch is on the doorframe (**6-52**). The wires from the switch are run inside the wall. There are a number of sensors available for garage door installation. One is shown in **6-53**. Sliding glass doors also may be protected by surface-mounting a magnet on the door and the switch on the doorframe (**6-54**).

There are sensors available for use on door galss that will detect any glass breakage. The sensor is mounted on the glass (**6-55**). The magnet and switch are mounted in the edge of the door and the door frame.

Hard-wired systems are installed at the same time as the house is built. The wires to doors and windows are run in the wall cavities in the same manner as the electric wiring is normally run. After the drywall has been put up, access to the wall cavities becomes greatly limited, and system installation becomes much more difficult.

6-51 The concealed magnet is not noticeable even when the door is open.

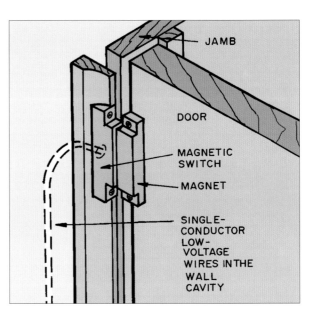

6-52 Some older alarm systems use surface-mounted switches. They are not decorative and are best hidden by draperies or shades whenever possible.

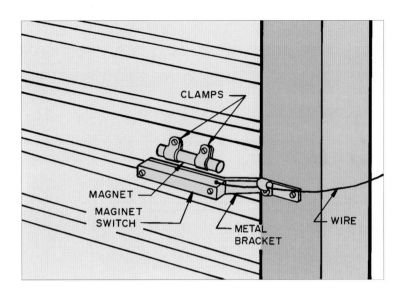

6-53 (Right) This hard-wired alarm sensor is designed for use on a garage door.

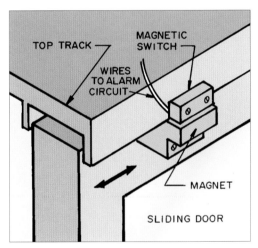

6-54 Sliding doors may have a magnetic switch mounted on the track and a magnet on the sliding door.

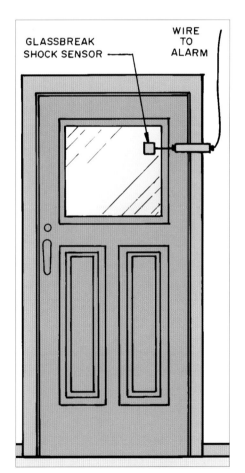

6-55 (Right) For warning of and protection against glass breakage, use a shock sensor on the glass that connects to a sending device triggering an alarm.

6-56 The central control station of a wireless security system. The transformer above the unit on the right supplies the 14 volts needed to operate the station.

WIRELESS ALARM SYSTEMS

The **wireless alarm system** operates on 14 volts from an ordinary 120-volt electricity outlet. The system has a central control station that has a transformer, which steps down the house current to the required 14 volts (**6-56**). Remote sensors are mounted on the doors and windows (**6-57**). These sensors are connected to a transmitter that is typically powered by a 9-volt battery (**6-57**). The alarm sytem is thus wireless since the transmitter needs no physical connection to the central control station.

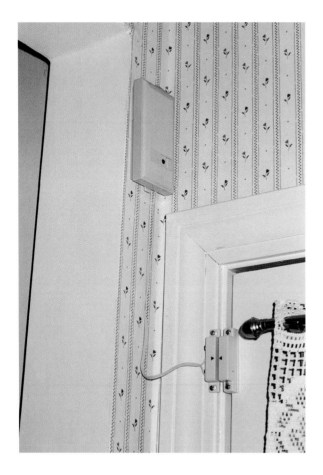

6-57 The sensor is mounted on the door and is connected to the transmitter by a small wire. When the door is open, the sensor activates the transmitter that sends a signal through the air to the control station, thus activating the alarm.

6-58 When the alarm is activated, an inside alarm and an outside siren sound a warning.

As with the hard-wired system, the alarm can be connected to the local police station or can simply activate an alarm inside the house and, perhaps, a siren outside (**6-58**). This system also can operate medical alarms, smoke monitors, and glass-breakage sensors. This system is installed after the house is built. The sensors are mounted on the door and window casing and the door and window stile (**6-57**). Installation on sliding glass doors is shown in **6-59**. One transmitter can operate on two doors if they are reasonably close together.

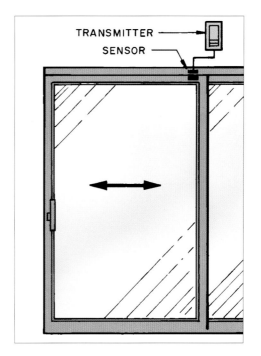

6-59 (Right) Sliding doors can be secured with the wireless-system sensor and transmitter.

CHAPTER 7

Installing Interior Doors

Hanging doors involves the careful construction of the rough opening including proper sizing and getting members level and plumb (7-1). Another consideration is the hand of the door. This refers to the side to receive the hinge and the direction in which the door swings. A well-hung door will have a uniform crack between it and the doorframe and will remain in any position it is placed. For example, if a door will not stay open, either the frame or the wall is leaning in a way that makes it move toward the door opening. This is very inconvenient. The positioning of the hinges and lockset are critical to a satisfactory installation. Everything must line up to produce a smooth, easy-to-use, well-operating door.

DETERMINING THE HAND OF A DOOR

In new construction the architectural drawing will show which way the door is to swing and which side will have the hinges. When ordering prehung doors (doors installed in the frame by the manufacturer) specify the hand of the door. In some areas there are different ways to specify the hand. Consult the manufacturer's literature before you order so that what is delivered is what is needed. One commonly used system for identifying the hand of wood doors is shown in 7-2. This system requires the door be viewed from the "outside." For example, you view a bedroom door from the hall to determine the hand. An exterior door is viewed from outside the building.

7-1 The framing carpenters frame the rough opening for interior doors. But before installation of a door, the framing must be checked for size as well as whether the opening is level, plumb, and square.

When you view the door from the outside, the right- and left-hand doors will **swing away** from you. If the hinges are on the right side, it is a right-hand door. However, if the door swings out toward you, as into the hall or a porch, it is designated as a **reverse door**. Thus, in this case if the hinges are on the right side, it is a **right-hand reverse door.**

CHECKING THE ROUGH OPENING

The framing carpenters frame the openings for the interior doors, as seen in **7-1**. They must make the openings the correct size so the doorframe and the door can be installed. The framing must also be checked for level, plumb, and square (**7-3**).

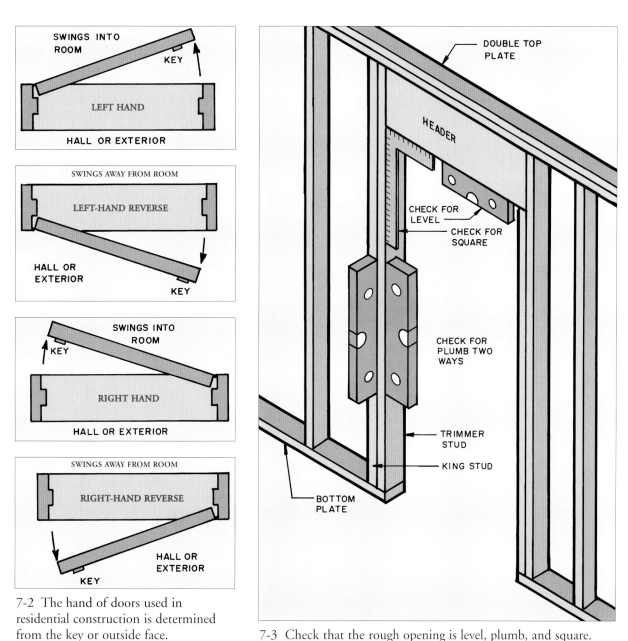

7-2 The hand of doors used in residential construction is determined from the key or outside face.

7-3 Check that the rough opening is level, plumb, and square.

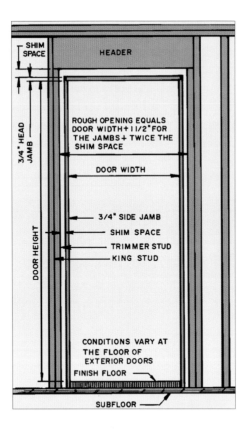

SHIM SPACE

HEADER

3/4" HEAD JAMB

ROUGH OPENING EQUALS DOOR WIDTH + 1 1/2" FOR THE JAMBS + TWICE THE SHIM SPACE

DOOR WIDTH

DOOR HEIGHT

3/4" SIDE JAMB

SHIM SPACE

TRIMMER STUD

KING STUD

CONDITIONS VARY AT THE FLOOR OF EXTERIOR DOORS

FINISH FLOOR

SUBFLOOR

7-4 Check the size of the rough opening to be sure the doorframe will have room to be installed, leveled, and plumbed. This is a typical layout for an interior door.

Also check the rough opening for the width between the trimmer studs and the floor to header height (7-4). The opening should be sized as recommended by the door manufacturer. If the manufacturers information is not available, carpenters often will frame the opening ½ to 1½ inches (12 to 38mm) wider than the overall outside width of the doorframe. Since the ¾-inch (19mm)-thick frame will not be on the job but the door size is shown on the architectural drawings, add 1½ inches (38mm) to the width of the door to get the overall outside dimension for the frame. Then add ½ to 1½ inches (13 to 38mm) for a shim space. The size of the shim space depends on the choice of the carpenter. These measurements apply to single interior doors.

7-5 This prehung door is protected with heavy cardboard edges.

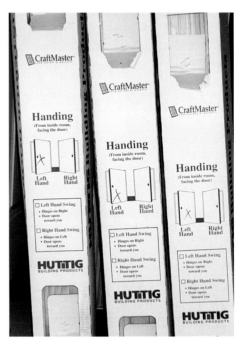

7-6 Some manufacturers print instructions on the protective cardboard covering.

PREPARING TO INSTALL INTERIOR DOORS

The doors are installed after the drywall has been hung and taped. Do not move doors and frames into the house until the drywall-taping compound has completely dried and the excess moisture in the air has disappeared. The drywall mess on the floor should be removed, as should all other debris before bringing the units in. Then sweep the subfloor so it is clean. Only then can the doors and frames be brought into the house. They should be installed immediately after being delivered. If they arrive early, store them in a clean, warm, dry, well-ventilated space. Place flat so they do not warp and cover to protect them from dust. Keep the doors away from direct sunlight or near any type of space heater. Handle the door with care so it does not become damaged or have fingerprints on it.

Prehung doors are carefully packed for shipment to the building supply dealer and then on to the building site (7-5). On the edges of the protective carton often there are instructions from the manufacturer for proper handing (7-6). After the protective covering is removed the casing molding is exposed (7-7). Care must be taken to not damage the molding or side jambs as they rest on the floor.

A typical prehung interior door and frame are illustrated in 7-8. This example has a temporary brace on the bottom to tie the side jambs together. Some manufacturers use short strips on the edge of the assembled unit (7-9).

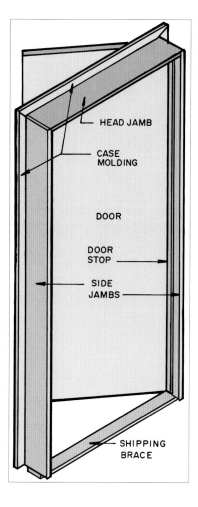

7-8 A typical prehung interior door unit has an assembled frame, casing, and door. The casing is nailed on one side. The casing for the other side is shipped unattached and is installed after the unit is set in the door opening.

7-7 After the protective covering has been removed, handle the unit carefully so the bottom of the casing molding and side jambs are not damaged.

7-9 Manufacturers add bracing to the prehung jambs to strengthen the unit for shipping.

TABLE 7-1 WHAT TO NOTE WHEN ORDERING PREHUNG INTERIOR DOORS

Interior Door Specifications

Type of door
design of door
surface material of door
core construction

Dimensions of door
door size
door thickness

Door jamb
type of jamb
width of jamb

Door casing
type of casing
size of casing

Hand of door

INSTALLING PREHUNG INTERIOR DOORS

Prehung interior doors are available for almost every common type of interior door, including swinging, bifold, and bipass doors. They can be installed quickly with a few basic tools.

A typical prehung swinging interior door is shown earlier in 7-8. The unit consists of an assembled frame with the door hung on it. Most types have the casing nailed on one side. The precut casing pieces for the other side are included.

Some prehung units come with the frame unassembled, but the hinges are installed on the side jamb and door. Often the casing molding is installed on the jamb. Another product is simply a knocked-down doorframe that is assembled on the job. The door must be installed after the frame is in place. Kits containing precut casing molding are also available.

Another type of prehung door uses a **split jamb.** A split jamb comes in two sections with the casing molding mounted on each (7-10). The larger main jamb has the door installed on it. This is nailed in place and then the other half of the jamb is installed from the other side (7-11). The split jamb has the advantage of giving some allowance for walls of various thicknesses.

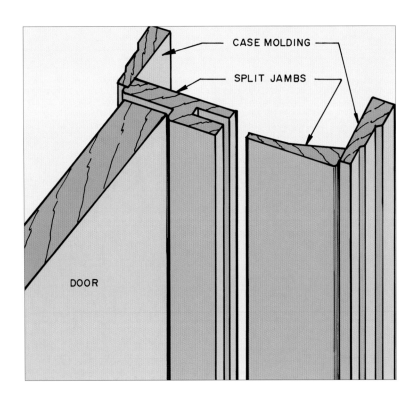

CASE MOLDING

SPLIT JAMBS

DOOR

7-10 A split jamb has two sections, each installed from the opposite side of the door opening.

ORDERING PREHUNG INTERIOR DOORS

When ordering a prehung interior door, be certain to note the specifications that are listed in **Table 7-1**. The more complete you can be in specifying your interior door, then the more likely you are to have the product you want. Designating the hand of the door is important.

INSTALLING HOLLOW-CORE PREHUNG DOORS

Hollow-core doors are lighter and easier to install than heavy solid-core doors. Begin by checking the rough opening for size and making sure that the opening is level, plumb, and square, as described earlier in this chapter on pages 93 and 94.

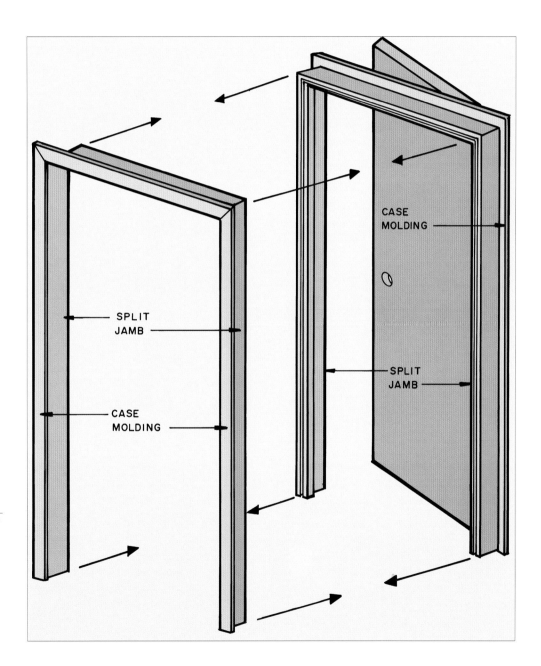

7-11 Each half of a split jamb prehung door unit is installed from the opposite side of the rough opening.

If the jamb is a little out of plumb, this can be corrected with shims. If the wall leans into the room, the door will always hang open or will not stay open depending upon which way the wall leans. This requires a major readjustment of the plumb of the wall in that direction.

When checking the rough opening, often you will notice that the opening is skewed, forming a rhombus (7-12). Another skewed condition is that the trimmer studs are out of plumb but in opposite directions. This is commonly referred to as scissoring (7-13). The amount that the opening is out of square will determine what steps must be taken to correct it. If the opening is found to be out of plumb by only a small amount, say ¼ to ⅜ inch (6 to 9mm), it is often possible to fit the doorframe in the opening and shim it so it can be nailed firmly to the trimmer in a plumb position.

While many unexpected things occur when installing a prehung door, the following procedure presents the basic steps.

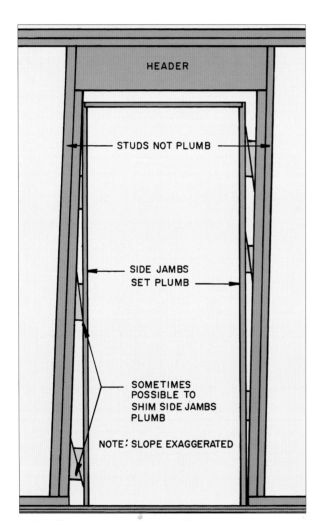

7-12 This rough opening has the studs leaning to one side to form a rhombus. The side jambs can be set plumb by shimming, if the studs are not out of plumb very much.

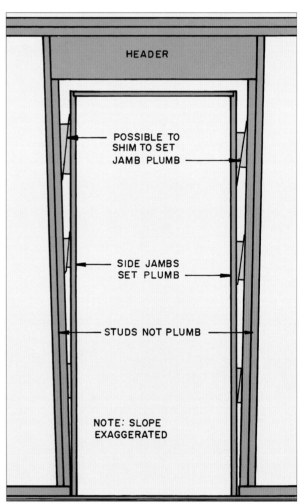

7-13 The studs on this rough opening are out of plumb and sloping in opposite directions. If the slope is not too large, the doorframe can be set plumb and secured with shims.

Begin installation by first removing any temporary fasteners the manufacturer used to support the unit while it was being shipped. Then place the frame with the hung door in the rough opening (7-14). Be certain the door chosen is the correct one. Check the type, design, and hand of the door. Center the door in the opening by setting the bottom in first and leaning it up so the casing is against the drywall (7-15). Hold a level against the casing on the hinge side and move the frame until it is plumb (7-16). Use a prybar under the door to balance the prehung-door assembly in the opening.

Some installers raise the bottom of the side jambs about ⅜ inch (10mm) above the subfloor if carpet is to be laid and ¾ inch (19mm) if wood flooring is to be used. This permits the carpet layer to tuck the carpet beneath the jamb and the wood flooring to slide under it. To get these heights, place a small piece of wood below the side jambs at the floor before nailing the unit in place.

With the doorframe in place against the wall and plumb, drive a finishing nail through the casing a few inches below the corner miter into the drywall and stud. Use 7d (2¼-inch) finish nails. If a pneumatic nailer is used, the prybar will let you balance the door and keep it plumb as you drive the nail. If a hammer is used, place shims under the door to support it because you will need both hands to drive the nails.

7-14 Set the bottom of the unit into the rough opening.

7-15 Place the case molding against the drywall.

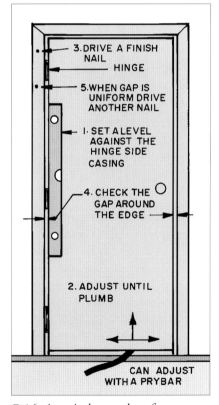

7-16 A typical procedure for securing the prehung door unit to the rough opening. Other techniques are used to get the same result.

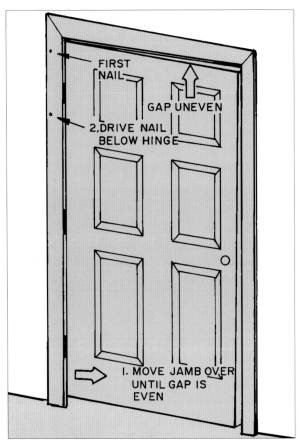

7-17 A small, uneven gap at the head jamb can be corrected by moving the hinge side jamb out until the gap is even and then securing the casing to the studs with a nail below the top hinge.

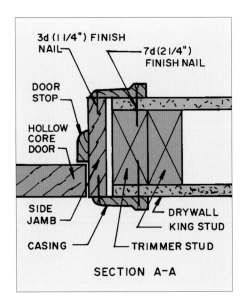

SECTION A-A

With the prehung unit lightly tacked in place examine the gap at the head jamb. This gap should be uniform. If it is not, move the hinge side jamb a little until the gap closes. For example, if the gap is on the other side of the door, as shown in 7-17, move the bottom of the hinge jamb a little to the center of the opening until the gap is uniform. Then drive a nail a few inches below the top hinge. Make any other adjustments

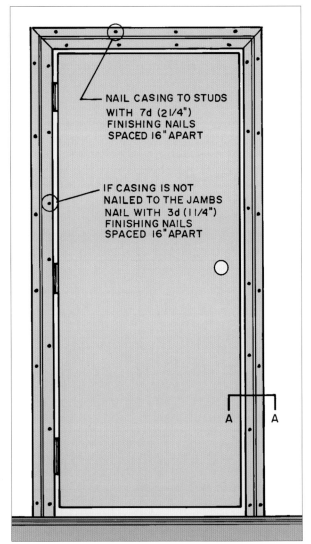

7-18 (Above and left) Recommendations for nailing the casing to the jambs and to the studs that form the rough opening.

needed in order to have a uniform gap around the edge of the door and the jambs. Swing the door to make certain it swings properly and will stay put in the open or closed position. Then nail the hinge jamb casing to the stud, placing the nails every 16 inches (406mm) (7-**18**). Match the gaps between the door and jamb to be certain they remain equal. Then nail the casing on the lockset jamb and head jamb.

It is a good practice to secure the miters with a finishing nail as shown in **7-19**. Some also glue the miter when installing casing to the jamb. After all the nails are in the casing, set the heads below the surface so the painters can fill the holes prior to painting (7-**20**).

At this point the door jambs and hinged door are securely in position. A decision must be made whether to shim the jambs or not. Some prefer to skip this with lightweight hollow-core doors and proceed to install the casing on the other side of the jambs, finishing the installation.

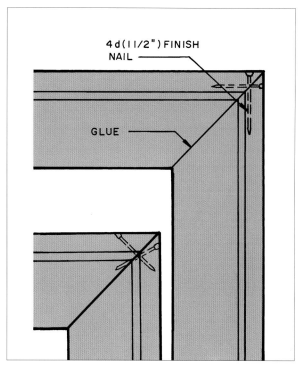

7-19 When installing casing on the jambs, it is good practice to glue and nail the miter.

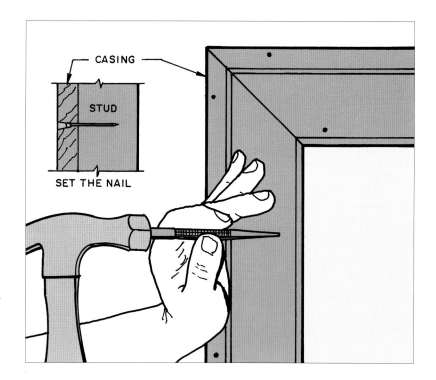

7-20 After the door has been installed, set the heads of the nails so the painter can cover them before painting the casing.

Others prefer to shim the jambs, thereby producing a stronger installation that is less likely to have a jamb to warp or bow. Should shims be used, place them behind each hinge and the lockset strike plate as shown in **7-21**. Shims are made as wide as the jamb and placed parallel with it. Do not force them beyond a firm binding position or the jamb may be bowed. Nail through the jamb to hold them in place. If the jamb has a slight inward bow, it can sometimes be pulled straight by tapping the shims a little tighter before nailing them. If it has an outward bow, it can be pulled in by nailing through the bow. Some install a wood screw through the jamb into the trimmer stud if the bow cannot be pulled up with a nail.

Some prehung door units are shipped with the casing supplied but not attached. Before installing these doors, nail the casing to the jamb with 3d (1¼-inch) finish nails as shown in **7-18**. If there is a danger of splitting the casing, a very small hole can be drilled; however, softwoods are generally used, so this is not a big problem. If hardwood casings are used, drilling would be a

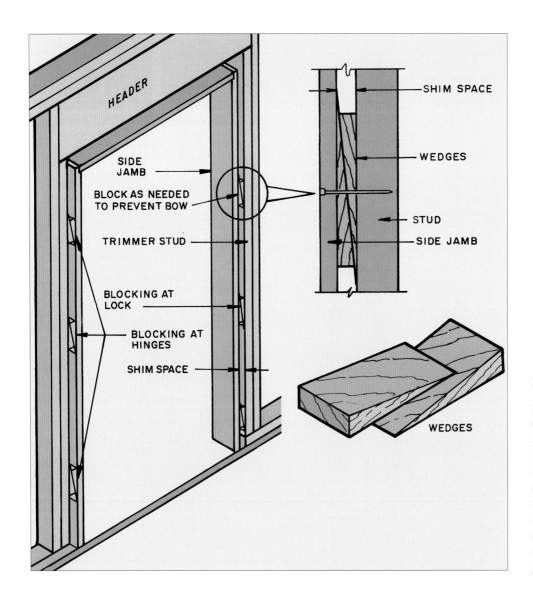

7-21 Whereas prehung hollow-core doors can be installed by only nailing the casing to the studs, adding wood shims strengthens the installation and reduces the chances of the jambs bowing.

good option. Be certain to leave a reveal (**7-22**) of about ¼ inch (6mm) along the edge of the side and head jambs.

INSTALLING HOLLOW-CORE PREHUNG DOORS WITH A SPLIT JAMB

A split-jamb prehung doorframe is shown earlier in **7-10** and **7-11**, on pages 96 and 97. Prehung-door assemblies with this type of jamb is installed in the same manner described for one-piece jamb prehung doors. Begin by installing the jamb that has the door hung on it (**7-23**). When it is plumb, nail through the casing into the stud with 7d (2¼-inch) finishing nails. Check the door swing and the gap between the door and jamb.

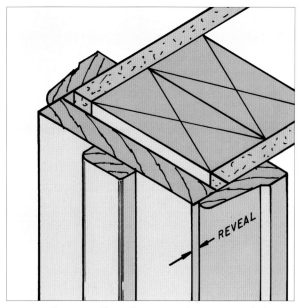

7-22 When installing the casing, leave a reveal along the edge of the door jamb.

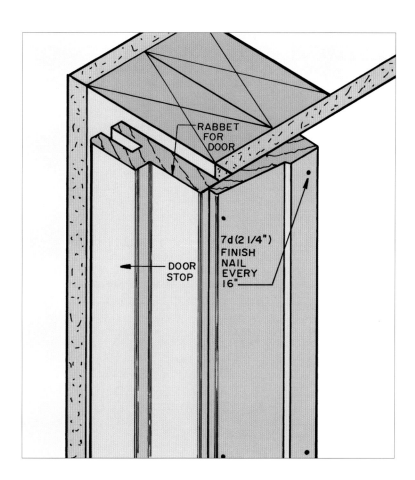

7-23 Install the half of the split jamb that has the hinged door attached. Use the procedures described for single jamb prehung doors.

Now install the second half from the other side (7-24). While hollow-core doors are often installed without shims behind the frame, shims will strengthen the installation and control possible bowing of the frame. If shims are to be installed, they are put in before the second half of the frame is installed. The installation would be like that shown in **7-21**.

Install the second half of the jamb following the same procedures as used for the first half. Some manufacturers recommend nailing through the doorstop, jamb, and shims into the trimmer stud (**7-25**).

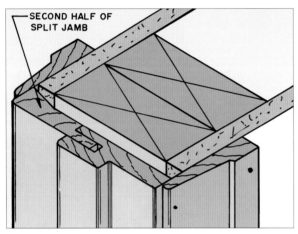

7-24 Install the second half of the split jamb. Shim the first half before installing the second jamb, if this is to be done.

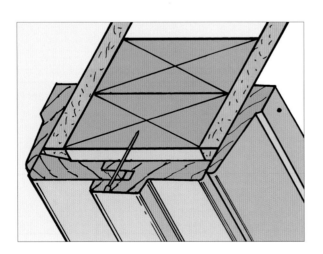

INSTALLING SOLID-CORE PREHUNG DOORS

Solid core prehung doors are much heavier than hollow-core units. They are hung basically the same way as described for hollow-core doors. However, the weight can cause the jamb to deflect, producing unequal gaps between the door and jamb; and eventually the door may rub on the jamb. What is required is the installation of shims behind each hinge and at the top and bottom of the hinge jamb. The lock strike jamb should have shims at the top and bottom and behind the lock strike. Refer back to the installation in **7-21**. Additional shims can be added as needed to level and plumb the doorframe.

Since solid-core doors are so heavy, some builders remove one screw from each hinge and drive a drywall screw into the trimmer stud (**7-26**). If the jamb needs some minor adjustment, tightening the screw can pull the jamb in a little. At first do not overtighten the screw but pull it up and keep the jamb plumb and straight. Check this with a long carpenter's level.

INSTALLING INTERIOR DOORS THAT ARE NOT PREHUNG

Sometimes interior doors are installed using a precut doorframe kit or by cutting and building the frame using stock lumber. The frame must be sized to allow the door to be hung to fit properly with a small gap on all sides. Provision must be made for installing the hinges, and sometimes the holes must be bored for the lockset. This is much more difficult than installing a prehung door. It requires careful preplanning and the installation procedure is a bit different from that described for prehung doors.

7-25 Drive finishing nails through the doorstop and tongues of the split jamb into the stud.

ASSEMBLING THE FRAME

Precut doorframes will have the side and head jambs cut to length and the head joint cut. This frame is then assembled by nailing the head jamb and side jambs at the corner (7-27). For a typical interior wall a 4½-inch (114mm)-wide jamb is used. This covers the 3½-inch (89mm) stud and the two ½-inch (12mm) gypsum wallboard finish wall coverings (7-26). If the wall is a different thickness, consider using a precut split jamb that permits some adjustment in the jamb width as shown in 7-24, or you can cut the jambs from stock lumber to the width needed. Nail a temporary brace between the jambs near the floor ends to hold the unit rigid as you prepare to install it (7-28). The doorframe is now ready to be set into the door opening. Again check to be certain that the frame will allow at least ⅛-inch (3mm) clearance on each side for the door and at the head and ½ to ¾ inch (12 to 19mm) or more clearance of the door at the floor. The floor clearance must make allowance for the type of flooring to be used, such as carpet or wood flooring. The bottom of the door can be trimmed some, if more space is needed, such as when carpet is laid.

7-26 Driving a screw through the hinge into the trimmer stud helps support heavy solid-core doors. This jamb is 4½ inches (114mm) wide so it covers the 3½-inch (89mm) stud and both layers of ½-inch (13mm) drywall.

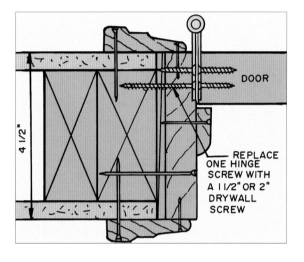

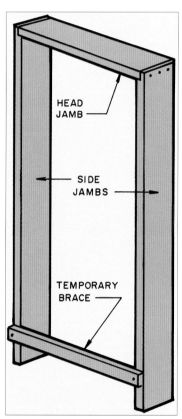

7-27 These are ways the head and side jambs are connected.

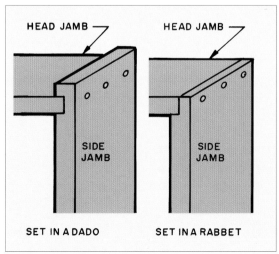

7-28 As you get ready to install the frame, nail a temporary brace between the side jambs to hold the assembly rigid.

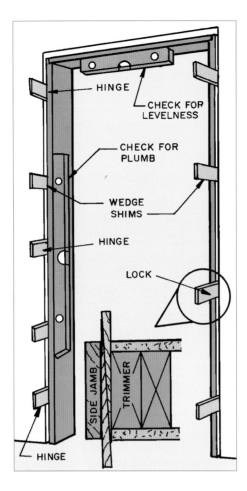

INSTALLING THE DOORFRAME

Check the rough opening for levelness and plumb as shown on page 93 in **7-3**. This will show if it is straight enough to accept the doorframe. Then place the doorframe in the rough opening (**7-29**). Place shims on each side as shown. Put shims near each hinge and where the lock is located. Shims near the top and bottom of the frame are also needed. Check the head jamb for levelness. Place a temporary shim at the floor if one side needs to be raised a little to bring the head jamb plumb. Check the side jambs for plumb. Lightly tap the shims together until they hold the frame in place. Do not over tighten, because this will bow the jamb. Now nail through the jamb and shims into the trimmer stud (**7-30**). The finish nail should be long enough to penetrate the stud about 1 to 1½ inches (25 to 38mm) (**7-31**). Use two nails per shim.

Now check the size of the door to see if sufficient clearance was achieved. If it appears to be too tight, plane some off the edges or saw some off the top or bottom. Do not remove more than ¾ inch (19mm) off the door, because the stiles will become too narrow and the door will be weak. When planing the edge of the knob side of the door, use the plane to create a bevel along the edge of about ³⁄₁₆ inch (5mm) to help the door swing clear of the frame (**7-32**).

7-29 Place the frame in the rough opening and shim to get it level and plumb. Place a shim behind the location of each hinge and the lockset.

Courtesy Senco Products, Inc.

7-30 Nail through the jamb and shims into the trimmer stud. Pneumatic-driven finishing-nailers are the fastest and easiest way to drive the nails.

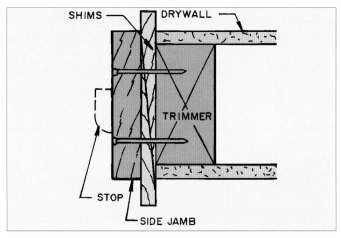

7-31 When the doorframe is level and plumb, drive two nails through each pair of shims into the trimmer stud. The part sticking out is cut off flush with the edge of the jamb.

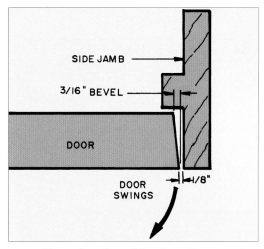

7-32 Plane the edge of the door that contains the lockset so that it has a ³⁄₁₆-inch bevel to help it clear the rabbet in the side jamb when the door opens.

INSTALLING HINGES

Hinges used on interior doors are **loose-pin butt hinges.** Exterior doors are fixed-pin hinges so thieves cannot pull the pin and remove the door. Residential-grade butt hinges are adequate for most doors. If unusually heavy or large doors are used, commercial-grade hinges are used. Review Chapter 6 for more information on hinges.

The parts of a typical butt hinge used to hang interior doors are identified in **7-33.** Some butt hinges have square corners. Butt hinges used on exterior doors have a fixed pin. Butt hinges used to hang doors are **swaged,** meaning they have the leaves bent so that there is only a small space between them when the door is closed (**7-34**).

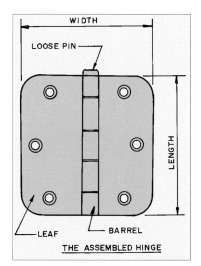

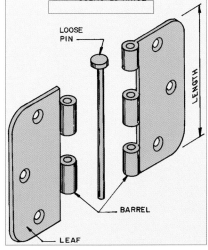

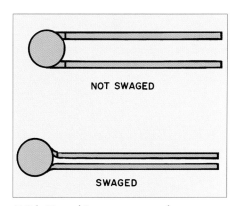

7-34 Door hinges are swaged, meaning that the leaves are bent in such a way as to reduces the gap at the jamb.

7-33 A butt hinge typically used to hang interior doors. Some have square corners. This shows a loose-pin hinge typically used on interior doors. Exterior door hinges have a fixed pin that cannot be removed.

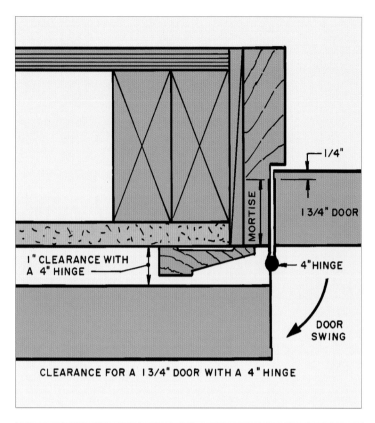

I/4"

MORTISE

I 3/4" DOOR

I" CLEARANCE WITH A 4" HINGE

4" HINGE

DOOR SWING

CLEARANCE FOR A I 3/4" DOOR WITH A 4" HINGE

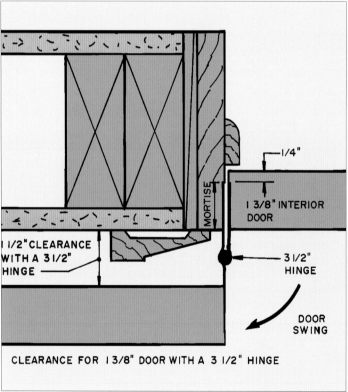

I/4"

MORTISE

I 3/8" INTERIOR DOOR

I I/2" CLEARANCE WITH A 3 I/2" HINGE

3 I/2" HINGE

DOOR SWING

CLEARANCE FOR I 3/8" DOOR WITH A 3 I/2" HINGE

It is important to choose the proper size hinge for the door. Notice in **Table 7-2** that the hinge size changes for various door thicknesses. The hinge must be wide enough to permit the door to clear the casing; so the type and size of casing must be considered as well. Mortise hinges installed on 1⅜-inch and 1¾-inch doors are shown in **7-35**. The clearance provided depends on both the hinge width and the door thickness as shown in **Table 7-2**. This is based on setting the hinge ¼ inch (6mm) from the back edge of the door, as shown for a mortise hinge in **7-36**.

Solid-core doors require three hinges because they are heavy. Hollow-core doors are lighter but they also have three hinges. The top hinge is located 7 inches (178mm) from the top, whereas the bottom hinge is placed 10 inches (254mm) from the bottom. The third hinge is centered between the top and bottom hinges (**7-37**).

NONMORTISE HINGES

Should you prefer not to cut mortises, use nonmortise hinges as shown in Chapter 6. Be certain to check the maximum load-carrying capacities for these hinges. It may be necessary to use four hinges.

MORTISE HINGES

With mortise hinges, one leaf is set in a mortise cut in the edge of the door (**7-38**). The other is set in a mortise cut in the jamb.

7-35 When selecting the hinge to use, the door width and the required clearance must be considered.

TABLE 7-2 SELECTING THE PROPER WIDTH HINGE

Door thickness (inches)	Hinge width when open (inches)	Clearance* of door from wall (inches)
1⅜"	3½"	1¼"
	4"	1¾"
1¾"	4"	1"
	4½"	1½"
	5"	2"
2¼"	5"	1"
	6"	2"

*Based on providing the hinge with a mortise stopping ¼" from the edge of the door. The specific clearance needed must be determined by taking into consideration the type and size of the door casing, which the door must clear.

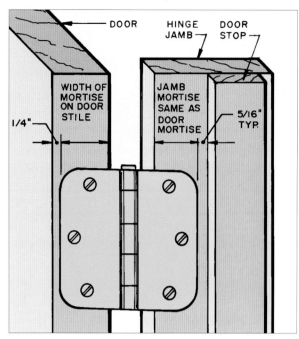

7-36 The hinge is set-in ¼ inch from the back side of the door. The mortise on the jamb is the same depth as the mortise on the door.

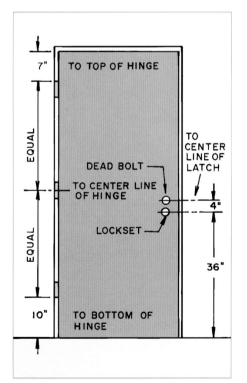

7-37 Typical locations for hinges, locksets, and dead bolts.

7-38 A mortise is a recessed area cut into the door and jamb into which the hinge leaf fits, setting it flush with the surface of the wood.

CUTTING THE MORTISES
IN THE DOOR

The fastest and best way to cut mortises is with a mortise template and electric router. The door is held with several metal door holders, which places the edge to receive the mortise in a position to make it easy to cut them (7-39). A mortising template is clamped on the door (7-40). The exposed opening is the size of the hinge leaf. An electric router is lowered over the opening and the router bit cuts the mortise, following the template and removing the wood inside (7-41). This leaves a mortise with rounded corners.

Round-corner hinges are widely used and drop into the mortise cleanly. If a square-corner hinge leaf is used, the round corner is cut away with a wood chisel (7-42). If a very small diameter router cutter is used, there is very little trimming needed at the corners.

When the hinge leaf is marked on the jamb, the width of the mortise must be the same as the width of the mortise on the door, as shown earlier in 7-36, on page 109. The mortise on the jamb can be routed with the mortise template and electric router shown in 7-41. It can be manually cut as described in 7-43.

The steps are shown in 7-43 for manually cutting a hinge mortise using a chisel and a knife. Begin by marking with the knife the edges of the leaf on the door or jamb and marking the thickness of the leaf on the face of the door. Use a wood chisel to outline the edges of the mortise and cut a series of crosscuts along the surface. Then use the chisel to cut away the area leaving a flat, smooth mortise. Should a round corner be needed, bore holes in each corner that have the same diameter as the hinge leaf. A one-inch hole is commonly used (7-44).

Courtesy Carey Template Company

7-39 The door is held on its side with door holders. This enables the mortise templates to be installed on it.

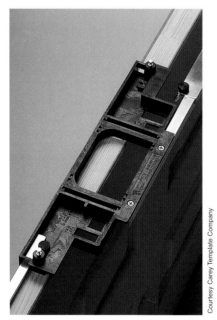

Courtesy Carey Template Company

7-40 Clamp the hinge mortise template to the door. Adjust it to produce the diameter of rounded corner needed. For square corners use a small-diameter router bit and clean up the corner with a chisel.

Courtesy Carey Template Company

7-41 Install the required diameter bit in the router. Lower it onto the template and follow the sides of the template. Set the depth of cut to the thickness of the hinge leaf.

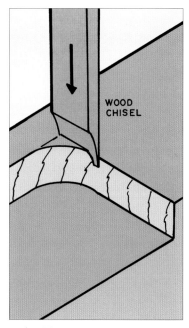

7-42 To get a square corner, cut away the round with a wood chisel.

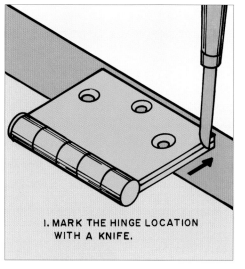

1. MARK THE HINGE LOCATION WITH A KNIFE.

CHISEL BEVEL FACING IN

2. MARK THE LENGTH, WIDTH, AND DEPTH. CUT TO DEPTH AROUND THE EDGES.

CHISEL BEVEL DOWN

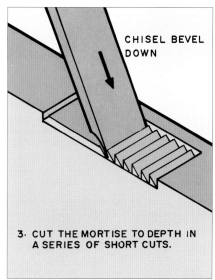

3. CUT THE MORTISE TO DEPTH IN A SERIES OF SHORT CUTS.

CHISEL BEVEL UP

4. CLEAR THE MORTISE TO THE REQUIRED DEPTH.

7-43 The steps to hand-cut a mortise for a square corner hinge.

7-44 If a round corner hinge is to be used, bore holes the proper diameter in each corner and remove the rest of the wood with a wood chisel.

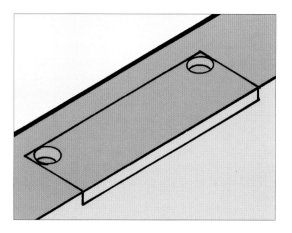

CUTTING THE MORTISES
IN THE SIDE JAMB

After the mortises on the door are cut, install the hinges on the door. Remember that loose-pin hinges must be set with the pin head on top. Set the door in the jamb. It helps if the doorstop is temporarily tacked in place to support the door (7-45). Locate the stop by measuring in from the front of the jamb the thickness of the door 1/16 to 1/8 inch (1.5 to 3mm) (7-46). When the door is in the desired position, mark the top and bottom of the hinge where it touches the side jamb (7-47). This locates the position of the hinge leaf on the side jamb and accurately locates the mortise in the jamb. Place blocking under the door to raise it to the desired spacing at the head jamb.

The mortises in the side jamb can be cut using the mortise template shown earlier in 7-40 and a router. Once the template is set for use on the door, it will provide the same setbacks as needed on the side jamb. Mortises on the side jamb can also be cut with a wood chisel as shown earlier in 7-43, on page 111.

Separate the leaves of the hinge and screw the leaves to the door jamb. Place the door in the opening, engage the hinge leafs, and install the pins. Check the door to be certain it swings easily. Make adjustments as needed.

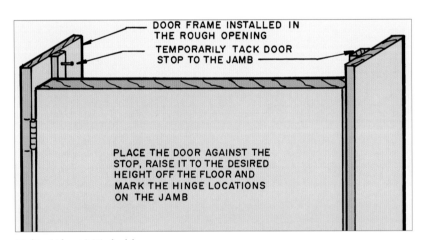

7-45 (Above) To hold the door as the hinge locations are marked on the side jamb, temporarily tack the doorstops in place.

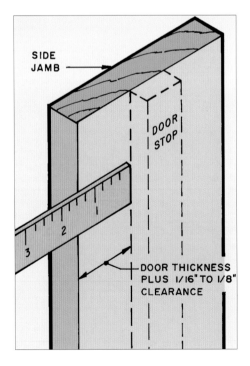

7-46 To locate the doorstops, measure in from the edge of the side frame.

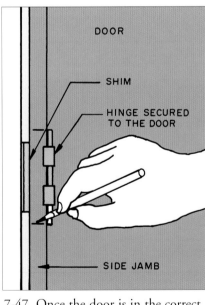

7-47 Once the door is in the correct position, mark the top and bottom edges of each hinge on the side jamb.

INSTALLING
THE LOCKSET

If the door that has been installed already has holes prebored for the lockset, this eliminates the tasks of having to locate them carefully and having to bore them. If the holes are not prebored, then you will need to locate them and bore. Use the template supplied by the manufacturer with each lockset. This template is used to locate the centers of the holes and specifies the required hole diameters. Typical instructions showing the steps to locate and bore the holes for the lockset are shown in 7-48. Always read through the instructions entirely before starting to install your lockset.

Generally the center of the lockset is located at a height 36 inches (914mm) above the bottom edge of the door. Exterior doors will often also have a dead bolt located 4 inches (101mm) center to center above the lockset, as shown earlier in 7-37 on page 109.

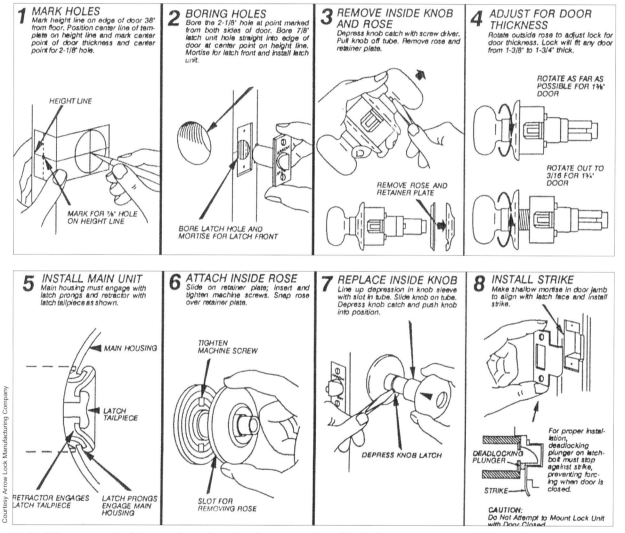

7-48 These are typical instructions showing the steps to install a lockset. Be sure to read through all of the steps that will be required before you actually mark or bore the holes and install the lockset.

BORING THE HOLES

When you bore the hole through the face of the door, do not bore all the way through or the surface on the other side will split. Bore until the tip of the bit just shows. Then finish by coming from the other side (7-49). Then bore the latch hole in the end of the door. A finished job is shown in 7-50. Boring tools commonly used are the expansive bit and the lockset bit (7-51).

INSTALLING THE LATCH & HANDLES

After the holes are bored, install the lock as indicated by the manufacturer's directions. A typical example of how the latch and handles are installed is shown in 7-52.

PLACING THE STRIKE

After the latch and handles are installed, you will need to locate and install the strike. The strike is installed on the side jamb. It is located opposite the faceplate on the latch and is set in a shallow mortise (7-53). Place the loose strike over the latch and carefully close the door. Hold the strike in place so the latch is centered in it and mark the top and bottom edges. Open the door and place the strike on these marks and draw around it on the jamb (7-54). This illustration shows how the mortise and opening for the latch can be cut with an expansive bit and wood chisel. Templates for use with a router are also another way to cut this mortise. Now install the strike on the jamb.

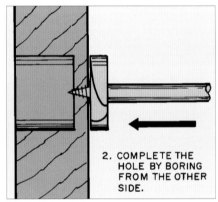

7-49 Bore the lockset hole from one side until the screw breaks through. Then finish the hole from the other side.

7-50 After the lockset hole is complete, bore the latch hole in the edge of the door.

7-51 Bits used to bore the large-diameter holes required for installing locksets and dead bolts.

1 — PLACE THE LATCH INTO THE HOLE IN THE EDGE OF THE DOOR.

2 — SECURE THE LATCH WITH SCREWS.

3 — PLACE ONE HALF OF THE LOCKSET INTO THE LARGEST HOLE.

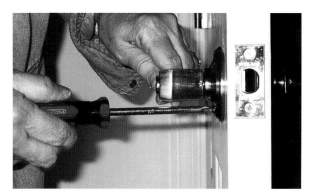

4 — INSERT THE OTHER SIDE OF THE LOCKSET AND CONNECT IT TO THE FIRST WITH THE BOLTS PROVIDED.

7-52 A typical example of how you go about installing the latch and then the handles and mechanism.

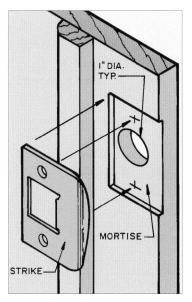

1" DIA. TYP.

MORTISE

STRIKE

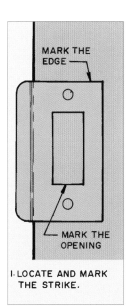

MARK THE EDGE

MARK THE OPENING

1. LOCATE AND MARK THE STRIKE.

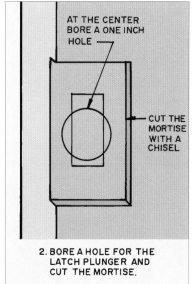

AT THE CENTER BORE A ONE INCH HOLE

CUT THE MORTISE WITH A CHISEL

2. BORE A HOLE FOR THE LATCH PLUNGER AND CUT THE MORTISE.

3. INSTALL THE STRIKE.

7-53 The strike is set in a shallow mortise.

7-54 Locate the strike and prepare the opening for the latch plunger and the recess for the strike.

INSTALLING
THE DOORSTOP

Finally, install the doorstop. Close the door so it is held closed by the latch being in the strike. There will be a little play, allowing the door to move some. Cut the top molding to length and place it lightly against the closed door. Nail it to the top jamb but leave the nails out some so it can be easily removed for possible readjustment. Cut to length and nail the side doorstops again, not driving the nails completely in place. Open and close the door. It must work easily and have a uniform gap around the doorstop. Adjust the stops as needed and set the nails. The stop should leave a ⅛-inch (3mm) gap between it and the door when the door is closed. This will allow for some movement in the door through the seasons (7-55).

INSTALLING
DEAD BOLTS

Dead bolts are installed similar to locksets. Use the layout template that comes with the lock and bore the holes as directed.

INSTALLING BIFOLD DOORS

Review the information on bifold doors that is covered in Chapter 4. While there will be differences between manufacturers in the hardware provided, the following examples are typical.

Install the head and side jambs as described earlier in this chapter. Be certain the head jamb is level and the side jambs are plumb. The bifold doors will not function properly if the doorframe is not true. Also be certain the size of the framed opening is exactly that specified for the door that is to be installed.

Begin by cutting the track that is installed on the head jamb to length. It can be cut with a hacksaw (7-56). Then install the track on the head jamb. It is predrilled and screws are supplied with the hardware (7-57). Install it on the centerline of the head jamb. Tap the pivots in the holes in the top and bottom of the doors (7-58). Be certain they are seated properly.

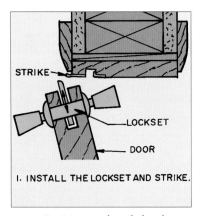

1. INSTALL THE LOCKSET AND STRIKE.

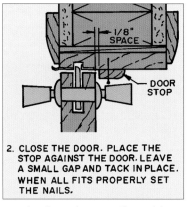

2. CLOSE THE DOOR. PLACE THE STOP AGAINST THE DOOR. LEAVE A SMALL GAP AND TACK IN PLACE. WHEN ALL FITS PROPERLY SET THE NAILS.

7-55 Position and nail the doorstops so the door closes easily and has a gap of about ⅛ inch when it is closed.

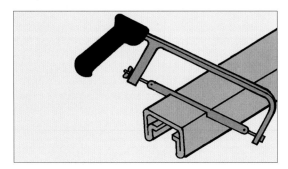

7-56 Cut the track to length. Make it ⅛ inch shorter than the width of the finished opening.

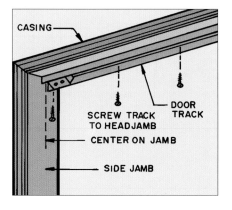

7-57 Screw the track to the head jamb. Locate it on the centerline of the jamb.

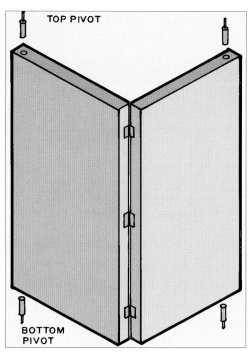

TOP PIVOT

BOTTOM
PIVOT

7-58 Insert the pivots in the holes in the top and bottom of each door. Get the correct pivot in each location as per the manufacturer's instructions.

CENTERLINE OF SIDE JAMB

JAMB BRACKET AT THE FLOOR

7-59 (Right) Install the jamb bracket on the centerline of the side jamb. It must line up vertically with the center-line of the track.

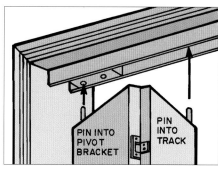

PIN INTO PIVOT BRACKET

PIN INTO TRACK

7-60 (Right) To install the door, lift it on an angle and insert one pin in the pivot bracket; then place the other pin in the track.

Next, install the jamb bracket at the floor (7-59). The center of the bracket must line up with the center of the track. It is fastened to the side jamb with screws. Insert the top pivot into the pivot bracket in the track and the top pin in the second door into the track (7-60). Move the bottom of the door over the jamb bracket at the floor. Set the bottom pivot into the bracket. Then screw it raising or lowering the door until it is the desired height and moves easily (7-61). If the door is not plumb with the side jamb, lift it out of the floor bracket and move it toward or away from the side jamb. When it is plumb, lower it into the slot on the floor bracket (7-62).

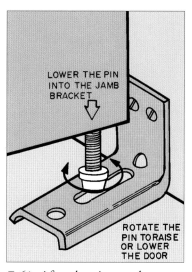

LOWER THE PIN INTO THE JAMB BRACKET

ROTATE THE PIN TO RAISE OR LOWER THE DOOR

7-61 After the pins on the top of the door are in the track, place the left side pin over the jamb bracket at the floor. Lower the pin into the bracket. Screw the pin, raising or lowering the height of the door as needed.

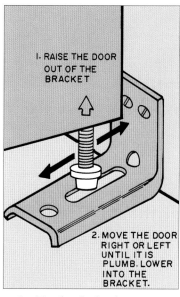

1. RAISE THE DOOR OUT OF THE BRACKET

2. MOVE THE DOOR RIGHT OR LEFT UNTIL IT IS PLUMB. LOWER INTO THE BRACKET.

7-62 To plumb the door, lift it out of the jamb bracket and move it right or left as needed and set it back on the bracket.

INSTALLING INTERIOR DOORS

7-63 This finished four-door bifold installation has door pulls matching those used on the locksets of the swinging doors.

Now add the desired door pull. It can match the pulls on the other doors in the room (7-**63**). If it is a four-door installation, add door aligners on the inside of the abutting doors about 12 inches (305mm) above the bottom of the doors. Adjust them back and forth on the slotted holes until the door remains tightly in line when closed (7-**64**).

INSTALLING BYPASS DOORS

Review the information on bypass doors that is covered in Chapter 4. While there may be some difference in the hardware provided, the following examples are typical.

After the head and side jambs have been installed as described earlier in this chapter, recheck to be certain they are level and plumb. Be certain the size of the opening is what is specified by the hardware and doors available.

Install the **track** on the head jamb (7-**65**). Locate it as directed by the hardware manufacturer. One example is in 7-**66**. Notice that the thickness of the door or panels to be used changes the location of the track on the head

7-64 Install door aligners on the inside of the doors. Adjust until the doors close tightly.

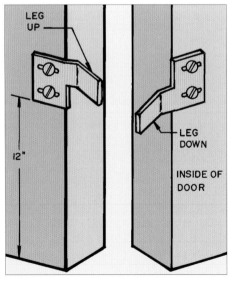

7-65 Screw the track to the head jamb as instructed by the manufacturer.

jamb. Now install the **door guide** on the floor. Be certain the center of the guide is lined up so the doors hang plumb (7-66). Install the roller brackets on the top of each door as specified by the manufacturer. The exact location can vary some, depending upon the brand. To install the door tilt the rollers up into the track, place the door perpendicular, and lower into the door guide on the floor.

7-66 Locate the track on the head jamb so the door clears the casing ¼ inch. These are typical recommendations for locating the track for two door thicknesses.

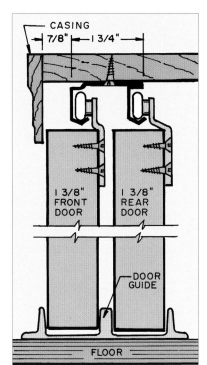
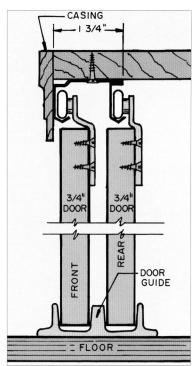

CHAPTER 8

Installing Exterior Doors

The installation of exterior doors has many steps similar to those required for interior doors. Review the material in Chapter 7 before proceeding with this chapter.

CHECKING THE ROUGH OPENING

The rough opening for exterior doors will have a header sized to carry the overhead load. This may be the roof and ceiling or the weight of a second floor. A typical header is shown in **8-1**. The framing carpenters frame these openings and must make them the correct size so that the doorframe can be installed. The rough opening framing should be checked to ensure that it is level, plumb, and square. Also check the width between the trimmer studs and the floor to header height (**8-2**). The opening should be sized as specified by the door manufacturer.

Exterior doors are available in several heights. For example, 6'-8" and 8'-0" doors are commonly used. Also exterior doors frequently will have transoms and sidelights, which will influence the size of the rough opening (**8-3**). The doors and frames will not be on the site when the exterior walls are framed so the carpenter needs information about each unit. Hopefully the plans contain a **door schedule** that gives the frame size and rough opening. When the unit arrives on the job (**8-4**), check the rough opening to be certain it will accommodate the frame (**8-5**). While the shim space allowed beyond the width of the doorframe varies depending upon the decision of the carpenter, it usually ranges from ½ to 1 inch (13 to 25mm).

8-1 This is a typical header spanning the opening for an exterior door. Doors with sidelights have a very long span and the header must be sized to carry the loads imposed on it.

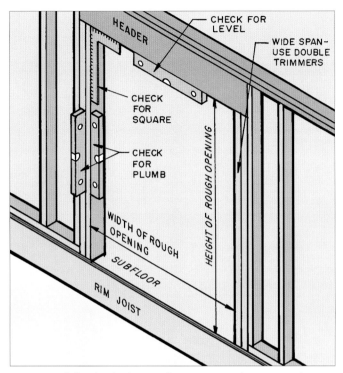

8-2 Carefully check the rough opening to be certain that the doorframe can be installed correctly.

8-3 This entryway contains a glazed fiberglass door, sidelights, and transom.

8-4 (Right) This prehung exterior door, with an assembled frame containing sidelights and a transom, is ready to be installed. Better check if the rough opening is the correct size.

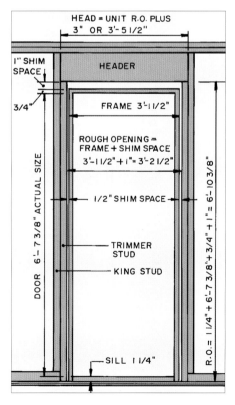

8-5 (Right) Typical rough opening data for a 3'-0" exterior door. The sizes may vary some between manufacturers and the sill design. Typical nomial 3'-0" × 6'-8" doors are actually 2'-11⅝" × 6'-7⅜".

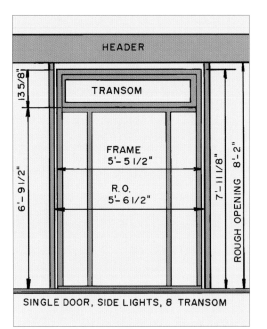

8-6 This is a complete entryway unit, including a prehung door, sidelights, transom, jambs, brickmold, sill, weatherstripping, and door bottom.

8-7 Typical rough opening requirements for a single door with sidelights and a transom. The actual size will vary from one manufacturer to another.

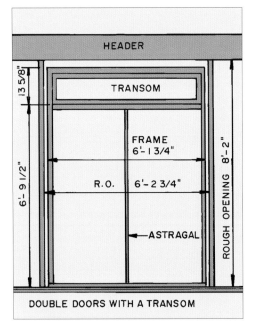

8-8 Typical rough opening requirements for a double-door entryway with an astragal and transom. Actual sizes will vary depending on the manufacturer.

8-9 This rough opening has been framed to hold the circle-top transom. Notice that the sheathing has been cut to fit around the curved top.

A complete entryway unit with a prehung door, continuous sill, sidelights, and transom is shown in **8-6**. The rough opening must allow for the transom and sidelight (**8-7** and **8-8**). The door and transom are installed in the rough opening.

The exterior wall sheathing is cut to fit around the curved transom or sized to fit on top of a rectangular transom (**8-9**). The sheathing fits behind the brick molding and clears the edge of the transom ¼ inch (6mm) or a little more (**8-10**).

Double exterior doors have an **astragal** mounted on one door that does not swing. An **astragal** is a molding joined to the edge of the stationary door to cover the joint with the edge of the operating door (**8-11**). It is typically ½ to ⅝ inch (12 to 16mm) thick and adds to the overall width of the doorframe. The astragal may be beveled or square, depending upon the edge of the stationary door (**8-12**).

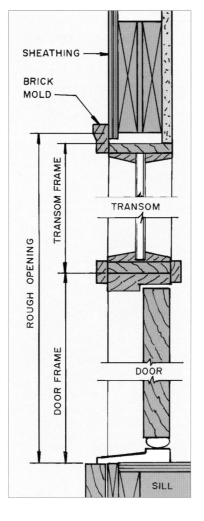

8-10 The transom brick molding fits against the sheathing. The doorframe plus the transom frame plus ½ inch equals the rough opening.

8-12 The astragal used depends upon the shape of the edge of the door.

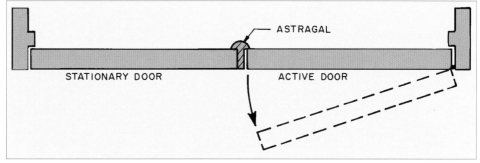

8-11 The frame for a double entryway door includes an allowance for the astragal.

When installing **exterior doors**, the type of sill must be considered as the height of the rough opening is decided. Some doorframes have a wood sill that rests on the floor joists or on a shim used to raise it to be flush with the finished floor (**8-13**). The example in **8-13** shows that the height of the sill above the subfloor is increased by the thickness of the finished wood floor (¾ inch) plus the thickness of the threshold to be used. The most frequently used exterior doorframe has a fiberglass or aluminum sill mounted on top of the subfloor (**8-14** and **8-15**). This adds the thickness of the sill to the overall height of the door. The actual design of this type of sill varies considerably from one company to another. This is only one example of those available.

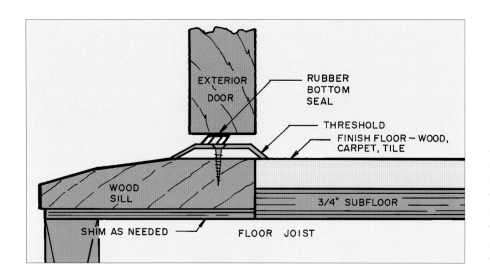

8-13 Some doorframes are made with a thick wood sill that is placed on top of the floor joist with the subfloor butting against it. These are not widely used.

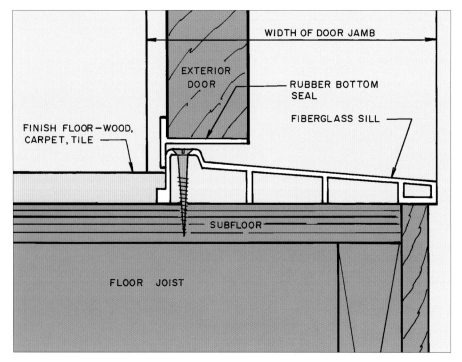

8-14 The most widely used sill for an exterior doorframe sits flat on the subfloor.

FLASHING THE ROUGH OPENING

After the sheathing is installed, the edges of the rough opening are flashed. There are several approved methods for doing this. The following example shows a method that installs a weather-resistant barrier over the rough opening before the door is installed and flashing is applied after the door is installed. This is used on doors having a brick molding.

Wrap the weather-resistant sheeting over the sheathing and rough opening (**8-16**). Cut it out over the opening, and wrap it around the side studs. Cut it flush at the top and at the floor (**8-17**). Then make 45-degree cuts at the corners at the top, about 9 inches (229mm) high, and tape this up out of the way (**8-18**). This flap will be folded down over the head flashing after the door has been installed and flashed.

8-15 This metal sill sits flat on the subfloor. Notice that the oak sill on the inside provides an attractive transition to the finish flooring of the interior.

8-16 Apply weather-resistant sheeting over the sheathing and rough opening. Cut out the door opening and wrap the sheeting around the sides of the studs.

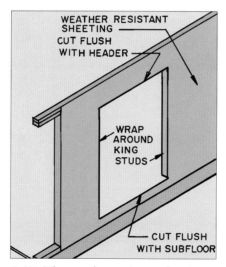

8-17 The weather-resistant sheeting is installed on the wall sheathing and fitted around the rough opening.

8-18 (Right) Form a flap at the head by cutting back a section of the sheeting. After the door is installed, it will fold down over the head flashing.

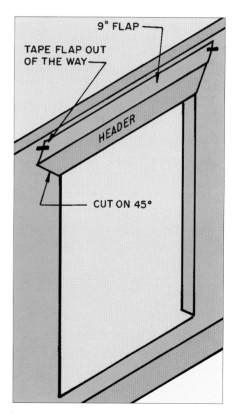

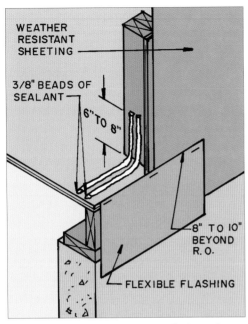

8-19 Staple a layer of flexible flashing from the subfloor to overlap along the sill.

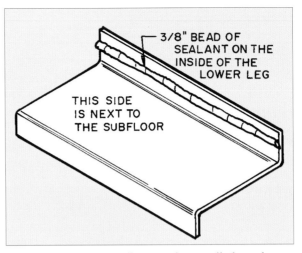

8-20 An aluminum sill pan to be installed on the subfloor between the trimmer studs.

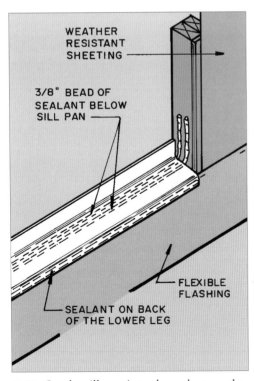

8-21 Set the sill pan into the sealant on the subfloor. Press the lower leg against the flashing. Secure with fasteners.

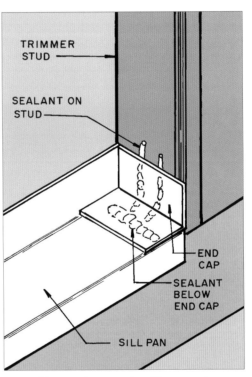

8-22 Place sealant on the sill pan and install the end cap next to the trimmer stud.

Now prepare the sill. Install flexible flashing over the weather-resistant sheeting at the sill as shown in **8-19**. Then lay two beads of sealant on the subfloor. Set the sill pan, shown in **8-20**, into the sealant and lap it over the sheet flashing (**8-21**). To attach the sill pan to the subfloor, drill holes for the fasteners, fill the holes with sealant, and attach the fastener. Then cover the fastener with sealant. Apply sealant on the ends of the sill pan, and then press the end cap in place (**8-22**). It should be noted that some builders do not use a sill pan. If a sill pan is not used, the door sill is mounted directly on the subfloor.

Next, install flexible flashing over the weather-resistant sheeting on the sides of the rough opening (**8-23**). Flexible flashing may be a two-layer paper product reinforced with a water-resistant compound, a polyethylene coating laminate, and reinforced with fiberglass, or a bitumen-type filler between two sheets of polyethylene or polypropylene. Lap the flexible flashing on the sides on top of the sill flashing. Then, install a strip of flexible flashing at the head, placing it over the side flashing (**8-24**). At this point keep the flap at the head up out of the way. You are now ready to install the doorframe.

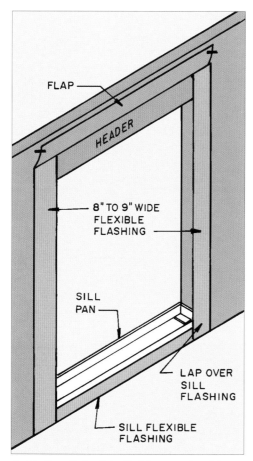

8-23 Install flexible flashing on the sides of the rough opening, overlapping the flashing at the sill.

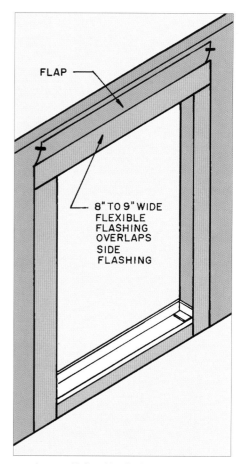

8-24 Install flexible flashing at the head. It should overlap the side flashing. The opening is now ready to receive the doorframe.

INSTALLING THE DOOR

The installation described has a door and frame with a brick molding that will be placed against the flexible flashing. Apply two beads of sealant near the inner and outer edges of the sill pan (8-25). If a sill pan is not used, apply two beads of sealant on the subfloor placing it so that it is near the inner and outer edges of the sill (8-26). Now run a ⅜ inch (10mm) bead of sealant on the back side of the brick molding. When the doorframe is set in place, this will seal it against the side and head flexible flashing.

Position the frame in the center of the rough opening, and lift and tilt it into the opening (8-27). With the sill in position on the pan or floor and the brick molding against the flashing, temporarily nail through the jamb near the top to hold it in place. Do not drive the nails completely in, because they may have to be removed for additional adjustments. Check for levelness and plumb. It may be necessary to shim at the floor to get the sill and head level. Check the side jambs for plumb (8-28). The side jambs can be adjusted some by placing shims between the frame and studs. Adjust until the frame is level,

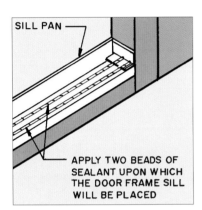

8-25 Before installing the doorframe, place two beads of sealant on the sill pan.

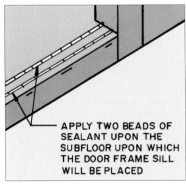

8-26 If a sill pan is not used, place two beads of sealant on the subfloor so that the front and back edges of the sill are sealed.

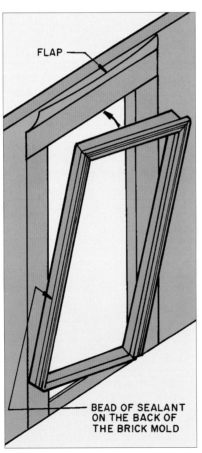

8-27 Set the doorframe on the sill pan and swing it into the opening. Press firmly against the flashing so that the sealant on the brick molding bonds to the flashing.

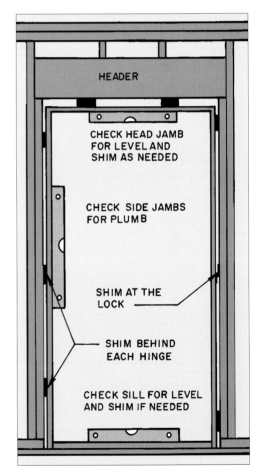

8-28 Check the doorframe for levelness and plumb. Shim as necessary, being careful to not over-shim and bow the frame.

plumb, and square. You can check for squareness with a carpenter's square, and verify by measuring across the diagonals (**8-29**). If the diagonals are the same length, the frame is square.

Remove any spacers in the unit that have been used to reinforce it for shipping. Swing the door to be certain it clears the frame and has a uniform gap along all of the edges. Adjust the shims until it is properly located. Secure the shims at the head and near the sill. Nail through the shims and jamb into the stud (**8-30**). In addition to the shims at the head and sill, place shims behind each hinge and the lock strike. Also

install three across the head jamb, unless the manufacturer's directions suggest you do not do so. Install one 3-inch or 3½-inch (76mm or 89mm) screw through one of the hinge holes into the king stud. When all is set, the brick molding can be nailed to the stud (**8-31**). Steel nails that are plated with cadmium, zinc, nickel, or chrome are satisfactory if they are sunk and covered with caulking. If visible, they are not recommended. Nonmagnetic stainless steel nails should be used, if they are to be left exposed to the weather. Magnet stainless steel nails must be sunk and caulked.

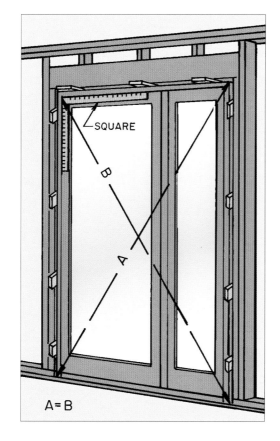

8-29 Check the doorframe for squareness with a carpenter's framing square and measure the diagonals. If they measure the same, the frame is square.

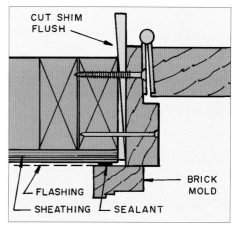

8-30 After the doorframe is set with the shims, nail through the side jamb and shims into the trimmer stud. Drive one or more long screws through the hinge.

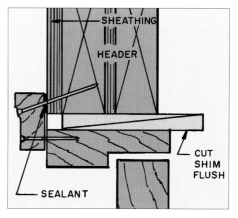

8-31 The brick molding can be nailed to the trimmer studs and header after the frame is nailed to the sides of the rough opening. Use nails that will not rust.

FLASHING THE FINISHED INSTALLATION

After the doorframe has been properly installed, place the required flashing at the head. This is usually aluminum or copper. Galvanized steel can be used, but must be kept painted, or it will rust after many years, or if scratched during installation (**8-32**). After the metal head flashing is installed, the flap of weather-resistant sheeting is folded down over it and sealed to it with a bead of sealant.

INSTALLING DOORS WITH A FLANGE

Some doors will have an aluminum or vinyl jamb and sill and use a nailing flange to secure it to the sides of the rough opening (**8-33**). The installation is much the same as for installing exterior doors with brick molding described earlier in this chapter. Review the material on leveling, plumbing, and flashing the frame.

Begin by checking the rough opening for size and flash it, as described for doors with a brick

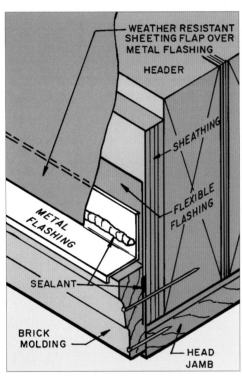

8-32 After the doorframe has been installed, apply metal flashing at the head and bond the weather-resistant sheeting flap to it.

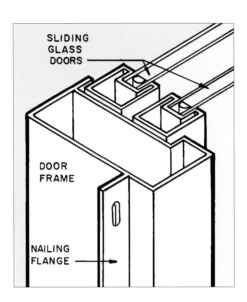

8-33 Some doorframes have a nailing flange that is used to secure them to the trimmer stud and header.

8-34 Place a bead of sealant on the back side of the nailing flange.

molding. When all is ready, begin installation by placing a bead of sealant on the back of the flange (**8-34**) on all sides of the unit. Some prefer to place the bead of sealant around the edge of the rough opening, being certain it is placed so that the flange makes full contact. The sealant should be placed so that it covers all the pre-punched holes in the mounting flange.

Set the sill on the floor and tilt the unit into the opening. Slip the flange at the head under the flexible flashing. Press the flange firmly against the wall (**8-35**). Temporarily install nails at the head. Check the frame for levelness and plumb. Be certain that the frame is square and that the doors operate smoothly. Correct any problems with shims. When you have the frame in the proper position with the shims, nail through the holes in the flange into the studs and header. Finally lower the flap of the weather-resistant sheeting and the flexible flashing over the flange. Seal them to the flange with a sealant, as shown in **8-36**. Additional flashing at the head is not necessary, because the mounting flange serves this purpose.

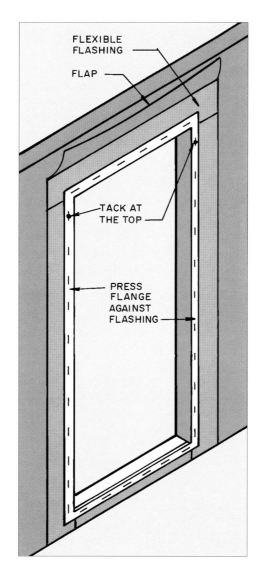

8-35 Place the doorframe in the rough opening. Press the flange against the flashing and nail temporarily at the top to hold it as it is plumbed and leveled.

8-36 After the flange is nailed to the trimmer studs and headers, lower the weather-resistant sheeting flap, and bond the flange with sealant.

8-37 It is a good practice to apply a layer of adhesive-backed flashing over the nailing flange sealing it with the weather-resistant sheeting.

After the door is completely installed, it is a good practice to place a layer of adhesive-backed flashing over the mounting flange (**8-37**). While this is not generally required, if plastic flashing is used, it does offer extra protection. In some warm, dry climates the flexible flashing is not used and the flange is nailed directly over the weather-resistant sheeting. In this case, it is required that adhesive-backed flashing be applied over the flange.

GARAGE DOORS

Garage doors are installed by technicians working for companies specializing in the sale and installation of these units. They know the capabilities of the various brands available and the unique problems involved in installing them. Drive units having ⅓ or ½ horsepower can be used on single- and double-car doors. A ¼-horsepower unit should only be used on single car doors. If the door is heavy, such as a solid-wood door, the ½-horsepower unit would be recommended.

First is the construction of the rough opening. As with other types of doors, the framing carpenters need to know the size door and the manufacturer's rough-opening requirements. In addition, there is a required wall space on each side for mounting the track and a minimum headroom between the top of the rough opening and the garage ceiling (**8-38**).

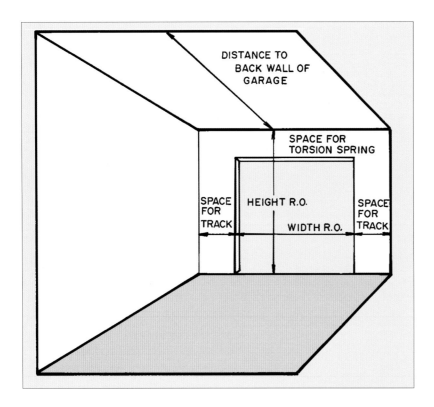

8-38 The garage door manufacturer will specify the minimum dimensions needed to install the door.

The door manufacturer supplies these minimum distances and installation instructions.

Garage doors require a wide opening, typically 8, 9, or 10 feet (2.4, 2.7, 3.0m) for single-car doors and 16 or 18 feet (4.9 or 5.4m) for two-car doors. These long spans require a header that will carry all of the overhead load, including the roof, garage ceiling, or a second floor (**8-39** and **8-40**).

The size of the beam must be determined by someone who is qualified with the knowledge of how to figure the loads and the load-carrying capabilities of various beams. The specie and grade of the wood used is a major factor in the strength, and therefore the size, of the member. Standard tables are used to find the size required for steel beams.

8-39 A wood beam was used to span this rough opening for a two-car garage door.

8-40 A steel beam was used to span this rough opening for a two-car garage door.

8-41 The exterior wall is covered with sheathing, which is then covered with a weather-resistant sheeting.

with brick molding described earlier in **8-23** and **8-24**. The molding at the head has a copper or aluminum flashing, as described earlier in **8-32**.

In warm climates having little rain, some codes permit leaving off the flexible flashing so that the brick molding is nailed directly on top of the weather-resistant sheeting (**8-42**). It is always best to flash the sides of the rough opening. This will give added protection over many years. Should the weather-resistant sheeting deteriorate years later, the flashing provides a second layer of protection.

After the rough opening has been framed and sheathed, the wall is covered with a weather-resistant sheeting (**8-41**). It is lapped around the sides of the opening and nailed to the inside. The opening can be flashed the same as for doors

The actual installation will require that you carefully measure the locations for each part. The **tracks** upon which the door rides must be spaced exactly as specified and be parallel up the wall and across the ceiling (**8-43**). The tracks are bolted to

8-42 The exterior edge of this garage doorframe is finished with a brick molding that seats on the weather-resistant sheeting.

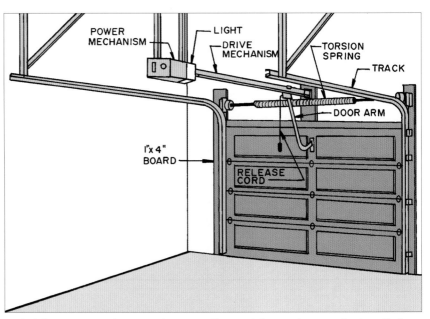

8-43 This is a typical garage-door installation. The tracks must be installed at the exact specified distance apart and be parallel their entire length.

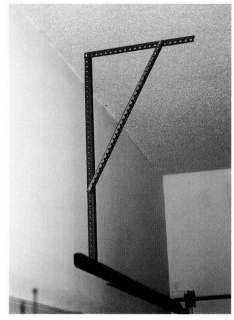

8-44 The tracks are bolted to the wall beside the rough opening. A 1 × 4 wood board is nailed to the wall on which the track connections are secured with lag bolts.

8-45 The tracks are hung from the ceiling with metal angle-iron carriers.

the studs alongside the rough opening (**8-44**) and hung from the ceiling with metal hangers (**8-45**). They must be hung the required distance from the top of the rough opening.

The **power unit** is suspended from the ceiling the specified distance from the garage wall and the proper distance below the ceiling so that the **drive mechanism** operates parallel with the track (**8-46**). Remember to plan to have a grounded 120-volt **electrical outlet** in the ceiling above the power unit. The **drive mechanism** is mounted on the wall above the rough opening and connects to the power unit. The spacing between these must be carefully measured.

8-46 (Above and right) The front of the power unit has a light that stays on a few minutes after the door is opened. The rear of the unit has the controls for adjusting the unit. Notice the electric outlet in the ceiling.

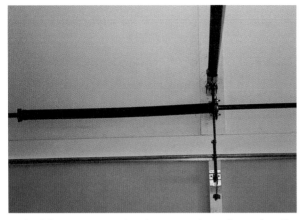

8-47 The torsion spring is mounted on the end wall above the rough opening.

8-48 (Right) The drive mechanism is connected to the door by the door arm. Notice the red cord that releases the door arm from the drive mechanism so that the door can be opened manually when electric power fails.

On the end wall above the rough opening, the **torsion spring** is mounted (**8-47**). Since it is under great tension as the door operates, it must be securely bolted in place. If you are replacing an old door, do not try to remove the spring. It is under tension and should be removed by a trained technician from a garage door company.

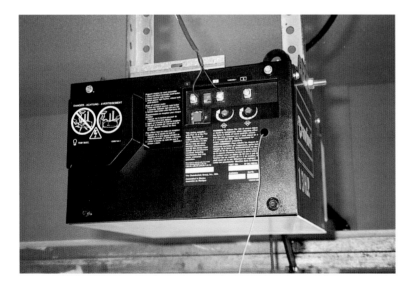

The door is in sections that have rollers on each end that run in the track. Place a section between the tracks and set the rollers in the track. Then, place a second section in place, and connect it to the first. After all sections are assembled, roll the door on the track to see if it runs properly.

Connect the drive mechanism to the garage door (**8-48**). The **door arm** is connected to the carriage that is moved by the drive mechanism. The other end of the door arm is connected to the door. You should locate the door arm on the door as directed by the manufacturer. It should be mounted securely with bolts. It is

---

8-49 On the back of the power unit are the controls used to adjust the operation of the garage door.

under great strain and requires a secure mounting. On the drive mechanism is a **limit switch.** It stops the door on the closing movement. Adjust it until the door closes properly. If the door hits the floor, it will automatically open. If the door does not seal at the floor, move the limit switch so it closes a little more.

There are controls on the power unit that regulate the force that is required to open the door and that are used to set the code for transmitting a signal to open and close the garage door from a remote transmitter (**8-49**).

THE EXTERIOR SIDING

Once all of the exterior doors are installed in new construction, the exterior siding can be applied. Wood, vinyl, and various composition siding materials are placed about ¼ inch (6mm) from the brick molding. This leaves a space for sealing the siding to the molding with caulking (**8-50**). When the exterior finish is mortared brick, the building brick extends out beyond the brick molding (**8-51**). A stone veneer exterior siding is shown in **8-52**. In **8-53** is a sliding glass door mounted with a nailing flange. Notice the space between the frame and brick is sealed.

8-50 Wood siding butts the trim around the exterior door; the gap between the siding and trim is filled with a sealant.

8-51 When mortared brick is the exterior finish siding, it extends beyond the brick mold. Notice the sealant closing the joint.

8-52 This stone-veneer exterior siding was placed leaving a small space beside the doorframe for a sealant.

8-53 This aluminum sliding glass doorframe has the space between it and the brick veneer closed with a sealant.

Another technique used for sealing a door with the siding is to install a wide board on the edge of the doorframe instead of a brick molding. This gives the door a wide decorative frame and increased prominence (8-54).

When the space between the doorframe and exterior siding is sealed, a backer rod is pressed into the space and then the sealant is applied. A **backer rod** is a flexible, compressive rod made from a foam plastic. It is placed in the joint to limit the depth to which the sealant can enter the joint and gives a firm support to the sealant so that it may be pressed into the joint and seal on the exposed surfaces (8-55).

INSTALLING HINGES & LOCKSETS

The various types of hardware used on exterior doors are described in Chapter 6. Refer to Chapter 7 for information on installing locksets and strike plates.

8-54 This door was framed with a wide board instead of a brick mold. It gives the door a decorative frame.

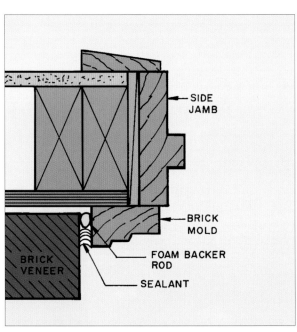

8-55 A backer rod is pressed into the space between the doorframe and exterior siding. It sets the depth of the sealant and provides a firm backing, making a more watertight closure.

INSTALLING ACCESS DOORS FOR PETS

There is a large number of access doors available for pets in a range of sizes to accommodate large, medium, and small dogs as wells as cats. These pet doors are typically installed in an existing exterior door but can be used between interior rooms or for access to a patio or basement. In some instances, it may be desirable to create a new opening in a wall just for the pet door, such as when you would like to install a pet door on both sides of the wall to keep out severe weather and drafts or to separate cat and dog access. Typically a dog access door is put in a kitchen or utility room door that opens to the exterior. Some homeowners choose to put a pet door in the front door of the house, but pet doors are available that can be installed in sliding glass doors, sliding screen doors, French doors, and windows.

SECURITY & PET ACCESS

Security used to be more of a concern before the availability of magnetic and electronically activated pet doors. The older-style pet door has a flexible plastic flap that the animal pushes on and that seals shut with gravity or magnets, and has an interior cover that can be locked in place to block access, such as when the homeowner is not at home. Electronic pet doors are activated by a special magnetic key or battery-operated transmitter that the cat or dog wears. This allows access to your pet while creating an effective barrier to strays, the neighbors' pets, other animals, or intruders. Some pet doors permit selected use, such as allowing the pet to enter but not exit, exit but not enter again, or locking all access.

CHOOSING A PET DOOR

When you are selecting a pet door, there are several things to consider. These include the purpose of the door, the best location for pet access, the nature of the house door, wall, or window into which the pet door is to be installed, and how the pet door may affect the functioning of a storm door. Some exterior doors may require special attention. Wood doors are easy to modify for pet door installation. Metal doors and certain fiberglass-covered doors may be hollow, requiring a pet door suited for their construction and the use of sheet metal screws or bolts not provided with the pet door. Panel doors may need the recessed area to be built up with wood battens or shims thick enough to make a flush surface for the pet door frame. Before you buy a particular pet access door, check the framing depth that the pet door will allow, the thickness of your exterior door, and whether the type of construction of your exterior door will work with the selected pet door. Be sure to follow the manufacturer's instructions for proper installation.

Shielding Exterior Doors

As a new house is planned or before renovations are undertaken, some attention should be given to providing shielding for the exterior doors. Wood, metal, and fiberglass doors are relatively energy efficient, but exposure to the weather can cause deterioration of the finish and, if not maintained, the exposed material can be damaged. Rain and sun that penetrate the finish on wood doors will cause great damage to the wood exposed. Metal skins will rust if the protective finish has deteriorated. Fiberglass door skins will resist damage even if the finish coating has deteriorated, but the appearance is ruined. Glass doors resist damage from the weather but proper attention to their frames is required over the life of the door. Many home owners and buiders use aluminum frames that are very good at resisting weathering.

Courtesy Therma-Tru Doors

9-1 Exterior doors that have large glass areas should have protection from the direct rays of the sun, especially if they are on the south wall of the house. These fiberglass sliding patio doors will resist damage from the weather but require a sun shield.

Another factor in considering providing some shielding for the exterior doors besides possible damage to the door unit itself—that is especially important for glass doors or other doors with glazing, such as French doors—is protection from the direct rays of the sun (**9-1**). This is important to help control the penetration of solar energy into the house in the summer that might otherwise make air-conditioning difficult or ineffective. Decisions on the need for such shielding will vary depending upon the geographic area in which the house is located.

SOLAR ORIENTATION & OVERHANG DEVICES

An overhang device, such as a roof overhang or awning, above a door will provide considerable protection. It is especially important on the south side of the house in the northern hemisphere because that side has the longest exposure to the sun. The east wall will get the low early morning sun and the west wall will get the low afternoon sun. The north wall will get little direct exposure to the sun. In the southern hemisphere, of course, it is the north side that has the longest exposure to the sun. In the summer the sun's rays approach at a steeper angle than in the winter (**9-2**). This permits an overhang to provide summer protection yet allow some sun to enter the glazing in the winter to allow some solar heating into the house.

This frequently used method of providing protection from the sun by extending the roof to form a large **overhang** is also shown in **9-2**. Large roof overhangs are commonly used in the warmer climates where houses typically have a low slope to the roof. In colder climates, where some solar heating may be desirable and roof angles are typically steep, the roof may have less of an overhang.

9-2 A roof with a low slope permits construction of a large overhang. A steep-sloped roof severely limits the length of the overhang.

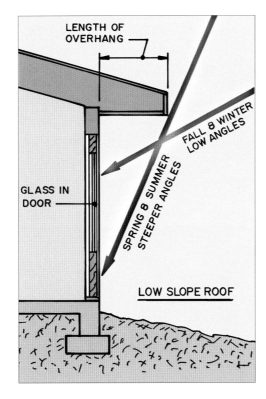

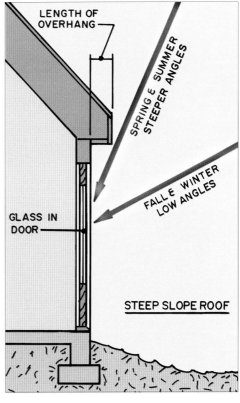

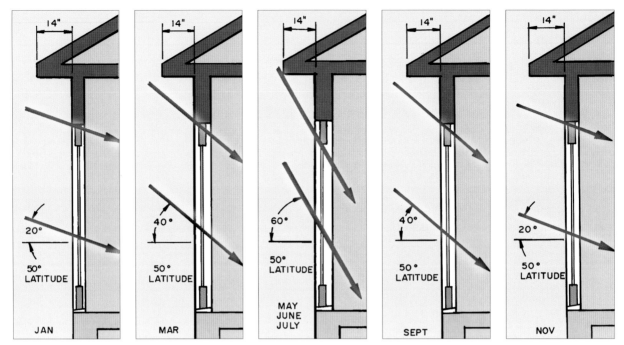

9-3 This shows the typical angles of the sun's rays in the northern part of the United States during selected times of the year. The same thing occurs in the central and southern states, but the angles of the sun's rays are different, depending on the latitude.

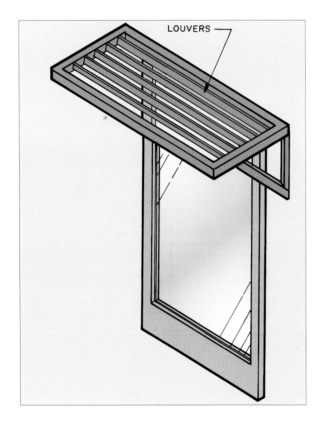

An example of the angle of the sun's rays on a house in a northern geographic region is seen in **9-3**. Notice that as spring and summer occur the angle gets much steeper. The same thing occurs in central and southern states, but the specific angles of the sun's rays are different.

If the slope of the roof is steep, a large overhang is not possible so a **louvered sunshade** (**9-4**) may be used. It is effective but does affect the appearance of the house. Consider making the louvers adjustable so they can block the sun's rays in the summer yet let them enter the house in the winter.

Another technique frequently used is to recess the front door into the foyer about 2 feet (610mm) (**9-5**). This, plus the normal roof overhang, protects the door as well as gives shelter to visitors entering the house (**9-6**).

9-4 A louvered sunscreen can be used to provide protection over doors with considerable glass.

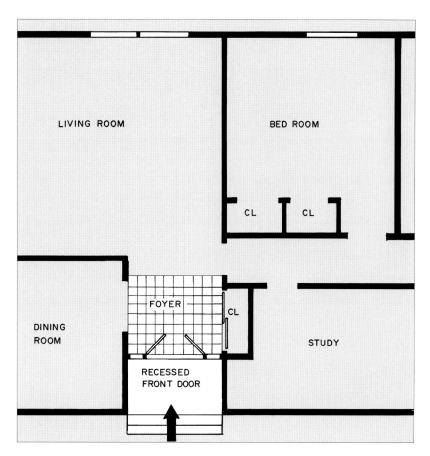

9-5 The exterior door can be recessed into the foyer, permitting the roof to protect the door and shelter those entering the house.

9-6 (Above and right) Recessed front entrances protect the door and provide shelter for those entering the house and are, as well, an interesting architectural feature.

Awnings are an excellent way to provide overhanging shelter of a door (9-7). One type is made with a fabric cover and can be folded up when you want the sun to enter or when the sun has passed on by the door during the day. Some awnings are aluminum and are permanently installed. Some awnings even have ventilation openings that release the heat trapped under them. This is an important feature because the air itself can get rather hot on a summer day.

Awnings are available in several colors. They do become a rather prominent part of the appearance exterior of a house.

Porches are a widely used solar screening device (9-8) as well as a very attractive feature, providing a protected outdoor area. However, wide porches tend to make the adjacent room dark because much of the natural light is blocked. Porches become a major part of the architectural style of the house. Notice the prominence of the various porches in **9-8** and **9-9**. Porches do more than provide solar screening and protection of the door from the weather. They also protect those at the door as they prepare to enter the house. On a rainy day a nice porch is a great thing to have on the entrance.

9-7 Awnings provide considerable protection from the sun and inclement weather. They can cover large areas.

DOORS & ENTRYWAYS

9-8 (Above and right) Long porches provide protection for the door and any windows in the exterior wall.

9-9 (Above and right) Porches can form a major architectural focal point for the front elevation.

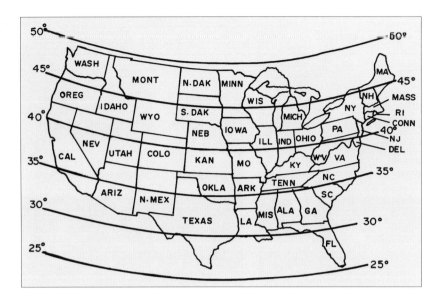

9-10 The geographic area of the continental United States falls with the parallels of latitudes 50 degrees to 25 degrees.

SIZING
THE OVERHANG

The amount of overhang needed to protect the door from the sun and the elements will vary depending upon the parallel of latitude, how it affects the appearance of the house, and how much shielding is wanted. Actually the decision becomes a compromise as these factors are considered.

The angle of the sun's rays is different at each degree of latitude and at any given time of day. The United States falls within parallels of latitude from 50° to 25° (**9-10**).

The length of the overhang, and the effects of the climate on heating and cooling, vary depending upon the location (**9-11**). In northern states of the U.S., the heating season is longer than in southern states and the introduction of solar energy is important. In the central and southern states the air-conditioning season is longer and protection from solar heat is most important.

The examples given in **9-12**, **9-13**, and **9-14** show how the geographic location will affect screening by an overhang. They are based on generalized examples of the sun's rays in each parallel of latitude. Exact angles can be determined if more accurate examples are desired. The penetration and screening of the sun shown is based on the use of French doors, sliding glass doors, and patio doors.

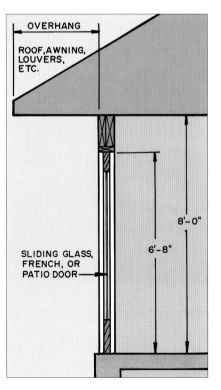

9-11 The length of the overhanging sunscreen is critical to provide the door with protection from the elements and direct exposure to the rays of the sun.

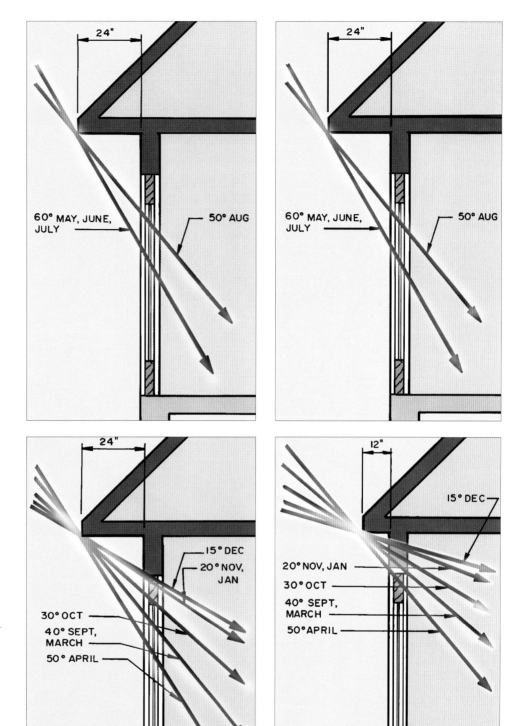

9-12 These drawings show the angle of the sun's rays during the year at the 50-degree parallel of latitude and how the overhang will control the penetration of the sun through glass in doors.

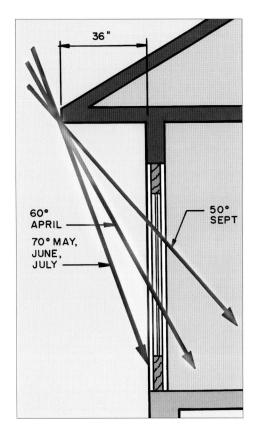

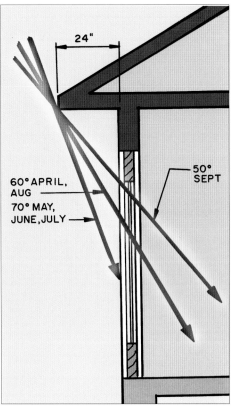

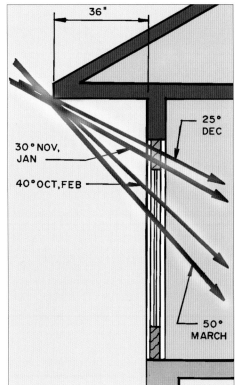

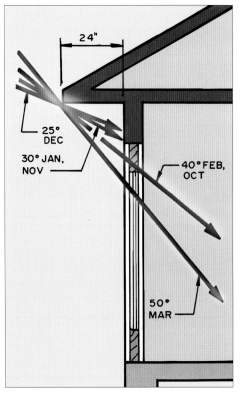

9-13 Along the 40-degree parallel of latitude the need for protection from the sun is about six months and the sun should enter the house to provide solar heat the other six months.

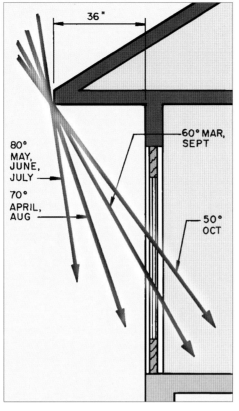

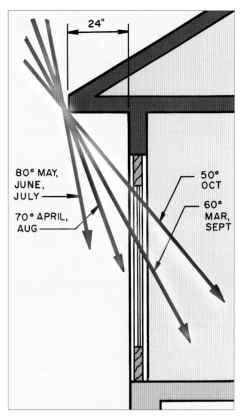

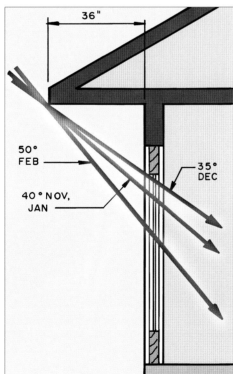

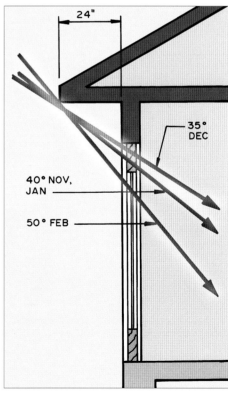

9-14 In southern areas of the northern hemisphere the air-conditioning season can be as long as eight months, so a large overhang of some type is very important.

To examine the overhang choices for a specific house in a specific location, make a scale drawing like those in **9-12**, **9-13**, and **9-14**, on the previous pages. Then project the angles of the sun's rays to show how much protection the chosen overhang will provide. Remember, many overhangs used will seldom provide total protection at all times of the day in all seasons. Usually additional protective devices, such as shades or curtains, are used to provide total control.

OVERHANGS IN NORTHERN CLIMATES OF THE NORTHERN HEMISPHERE

A series of examples for sun exposure in the 50-degree parallel of latitude are shown in **9-12**. The heating season typically runs from September through April. During this time the overhang should permit admission of as much solar heat as possible.

OVERHANGS IN CENTRAL STATES OF THE UNITED STATES

Examples of overhangs in central states along the 40-degree parallel of latitude are shown in **9-13**. Here the heating and cooling seasons are about equal, so six months protection from hot solar heat is needed and for six months solar penetration into the house is desirable.

OVERHANGS IN SOUTHERN STATES OF THE UNITED STATES

In the southern states along the 30-degree parallel of latitude the air-conditioning season can be as long as eight months, as shown in **9-14**, so that penetration of the sun's rays through the glazing is a major consideration. A large overhang of some type is needed. If planned properly, there will be some solar penetration during the short heating season.

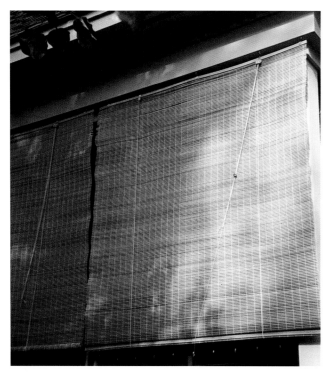

9-15 Bamboo- or reed-type shades on the exterior of glass doors provide an excellent sunscreen and yet admit some natural light.

9-16 Venetian blinds reflect the sun back to the glass yet can be opened to allow the sun to enter the room in the cold season.

OTHER
EXTERIOR SCREENING
TECHNIQUES

Sliding glass doors can have extra protection from solar penetration if some type of shade is used. Bamboo shades on the exterior work well (**9-15**). On the interior of glass doors, some form of venetian blind or rolling or pleated shade may be useful (**9-16** and **9-17**). Some pleated shades have several layers of fabric, forming a honeycomb shade that has increased insulation properties compared to a single layer shade. Draw drapes also provide some protection. Insulated draperies are available (**9-18**). All of these protective devices allow a certain amount of natural light to pass through, keeping the room from being too dark.

9-17 Pleated blinds effectively block the sun's rays. They are raised to the top of the door when the sun passes and will allow the sun to enter during the heating season.

9-18 Draperies are an easy way to enhance the room yet provide some control over the penetration of solar heat. Insulated draperies provide a great deal more protection.

9-19 The screen is a special sun-shading fabric that is placed on the outside of doors and windows. It prevents the sun from heating the glass and dissipates the heat before it reaches inside.

In areas of long summers the screens on glazed doors can be made using special sun-shading fabric if it is made of a strong vinyl-coated polyester. A sample on a window screen is shown in **9-19** and the completed exterior is seen in **9-20**.

In some cases a **fence** can be erected that blocks the sun at certain times of the day (**9-21**). While a fence such as this can block some of the rays of the sun and provide privacy, it also blocks much of the view of the exterior surroundings from inside the house. Fences work best on the east and west sides of the house because there the rays of the sun are on lower angles. Be certain to louver or stagger the board to allow some natural ventilation to reach the house. Another idea is to build a trellis and let vines grow over it. It provides some screening yet permits passage of air and natural light. Consider planting a row of **tall shrubs** or **trees** with dense foliage (**9-22**). In the winter deciduous trees drop their leaves and permit the suns rays to shine through, providing solar heat (**9-23**).

9-20 This house has the south wall glazing protected with a special sun-screening fabric, greatly reducing solar heat penetration.

9-21 (Right) Fences and trellises can provide some protection from the low angles of solar radiation.

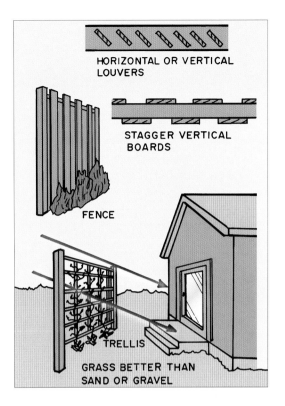

9-22 Shrubs or evergreen trees provide a dense sunscreen.

9-23 In the winter deciduous trees lose their leaves, permitting the sun to fall on the door glazing.

Courtesy Vista Solar Control Film from DPF Film

9-24 Solar glazing films that are applied to the glazing control the admission of solar heat.

SOLAR-CONTROL GLAZING FILMS

Solar-control glazing films are applied to clear glazing that has already been installed. These films are typically installed by trained technicians. They are an invisible film made with a laminate of polyester and metalized coatings combined with a clear, distortion-free adhesive system and a scratch-resistant face coating providing almost total optical clarity. They can be applied to single- and double-pane glazing (9-24). If the glass is broken, the film holds most of the broken fragments in place.

There are various types of solar-control glazing films available. Some are especially effective in reducing the passage of damaging ultraviolet rays and reduce sun glare. Ultraviolet light causes skin damage and damages the cornea, lens, and retina of the eyes. It also fades draperies, furnishings, and carpets. A low-E film reflects heat back into the room rather than allowing the glass to absorb it. This reduces interior heat loss through the glass to the cold outside. Another film will reject much of the exterior solar energy that reaches the door glazing, producing savings in summer air-conditioning costs.

Solar-control glazing films are available in several colors ranging from a light gray neutral color to gold, bronze, and silver.

As a film is selected, the needs for the installation must be decided. Is the reduction in ultraviolet transmission a major feature or the reduction of glare or heat transfer? For example, if a film that primarily reduces glare is chosen, it will have a low light-transmission factor. If the door faces south and the house is in a warm climate, solar heat rejection will probably be more important. The final choice will be a balance between visible light transmission, resistance to ultraviolet transmission, solar energy reduction, and shading and glare reduction. Manufacturers have extensive data on these factors for their range of film products.

Additional Information

The Window and Door Manufacturers Association is a professional organization representing industry professionals across the U.S. and Canada, including manufacturers, dealers, designers, products, etc. Related publications are available from:

Window and Door Manufacturers
Association
1400 East Touhy Ave. Suite G-54
Des Plaines, IL 60018-3337

Specifications for making buildings accessible by the physically handicapped are in the report *ANSI-A117.1*, produced and available from:

American National Standards Institute, Inc.
11 West 42nd St., 13th Floor
New York, NY 10036

The *Americans with Disabilities Act* and *Guidelines* are available from:

U.S. Architectural & Transportation Barriers
Compliance Board
1331 F Street N.W., Suite 1000
Washington, DC 20004-1111

Other trade organizations that may be helpful include:

American Architectural Manufacturers
Association [*Training Manual*]
1827 Walden Office Square, Suite 104
Schaumburg, IL 60173-4268

American Society for Testing and Materials
100 Barr Harbor Drive
West Conshohocken, PA 19428-2958

Canadian Standards Association
178 Rexdale Boulevard
Toronto, Ontario
Canada M9W IR3

Insulated Steel Door Institute
30200 Detroit Road
Cleveland, OH 44145-1967

National Association of Home Builders
1201 Fifteenth St. NW
Washington, DC 20005

Steel Door Institute
30200 Detroit Road
Cleveland, OH 44145-1967

Selected Bibliography

DeChiara, J., J. Panero, and M. Zelnick. *Time-Saver Standards for Interior Design and Space Planning.* New York: McGraw-Hill, 1984.

——— *Time Saver Standards for Housing and Residential Development.* New York: McGraw-Hill, 1984.

Merritt, F.S., and J.T. Ricketts. *Building Design and Construction Handbook.* New York: McGraw-Hill, 1994.

Peters, R. *Great Windows & Doors.* New York: Sterling Publishing Co., 2001.

Spence, W.P. *Carpentry & Building Construction.* New York: Sterling Publishing Co., 1999.

Spence, W.P. *Encyclopedia of Construction Methods & Materials.* New York: Sterling Publishing Co., 2000.

Spence, W.P. *Finish Carpentry.* New York: Sterling Publishing Co., 1995.

Spence, W.P. *Installing & Finishing Drywall.* New York: Sterling Publishing Co., 1998.

Spence, W.P. *Windows & Skylights.* New York: Sterling Publishing Co., 2001.

Sweet's General Building and Renovation, Catalog File. New York: McGraw-Hill, n.d.

Sweet's Group. *Kitchen and Bath Source Book.* New York: McGraw-Hill, n.d.

Index

Metric Equivalents

[to the nearest mm, 0.1cm, or 0.01m]

inches	mm	cm	inches	mm	cm	inches	mm	cm
⅛	3	0.3	13	330	33.0	38	965	96.5
¼	6	0.6	14	356	35.6	39	991	99.1
⅜	10	1.0	15	381	38.1	40	1016	101.6
½	13	1.3	16	406	40.6	41	1041	104.1
⅝	16	1.6	17	432	43.2	42	1067	106.7
¾	19	1.9	18	457	45.7	43	1092	109.2
⅞	22	2.2	19	483	48.3	44	1118	111.8
1	25	2.5	20	508	50.8	45	1143	114.3
1¼	32	3.2	21	533	53.3	46	1168	116.8
1½	38	3.8	22	559	55.9	47	1194	119.4
1¾	44	4.4	23	584	58.4	48	1219	121.9
2	51	5.1	24	610	61.0	49	1245	124.5
2½	64	6.4	25	635	63.5	50	1270	127.0
3	76	7.6	26	660	66.0			
3½	89	8.9	27	686	68.6	inches	feet	m
4	102	10.2	28	711	71.1			
4½	114	11.4	29	737	73.7	12	1	0.31
5	127	12.7	30	762	76.2	24	2	0.61
6	152	15.2	31	787	78.7	36	3	0.91
7	178	17.8	32	813	81.3	48	4	1.22
8	203	20.3	33	838	83.8	60	5	1.52
9	229	22.9	34	864	86.4	72	6	1.83
10	254	25.4	35	889	88.9	84	7	2.13
11	279	27.9	36	914	91.4	96	8	2.44
12	305	30.5	37	940	94.0	108	9	2.74

Conversion Factors

1 mm	=	0.039 inch	1 inch	=	25.4 mm	mm	=	millimeter
1 m	=	3.28 feet	1 foot	=	304.8 mm	cm	=	centimeter
1 m^2	=	10.8 square feet	1 square foot	=	0.09 m^2	m	=	meter
						m^2	=	square meter